LANCASTER COUNTY, VIRGINIA MARRIAGE BONDS 1652 - 1850

Compiled By
IDA J. LEE

CLEARFIELD

Originally published
1965

Reprinted
Genealogical Publishing Co., Inc.
Baltimore, Maryland
1972

Reprinted for
Clearfield Company, Inc. by
Genealogical Publishing Co., Inc.
Baltimore, Maryland
1994, 1997, 2003

Library of Congress Cataloging in Publication Data
Lee, Ida Johnson.
 Lancaster County, Virginia, marriage bonds, 1652-1850.
 Reprint of the 1965 ed.
 1. Marriage licenses—Lancaster Co., Va. I. Title.
F232.L2L42 1972   929.3'755'22   72-39382
ISBN 0-8063-0500-2

NOTICE

This work was reproduced by the photo-offset process from the original mimeographed edition. A characteristic of mimeographed copy—from which the offset printer must work—is that the copy is often very light and uneven, while at the same time over-inking may be present, such as, for example, when individual letters appear as a smear. Every effort has been made by our photo-offset printer to produce as fine a reprint of the original mimeographed edition as possible.

GENEALOGICAL PUBLISHING COMPANY

Made in the United States of America

LANCASTER CO., VA. MARRIAGE BONDS 1652-1850

DATE	GROOM	BRIDE	PARENTS
31 Jan. 1787	Alderson, John of Richmond Co.	Rachel Davenport	
18 Jan. 1802	Alford, John	Patty Jones	
8 Feb. 1811	Alford, Nathan	Nancy Bell	
15 Dec. 1775	Allen, Reuben	Hannah Bailey	
21 Dec. 1807	Arms, Walter	Betsy Tarkelson	
7 May 1809	Arms, Walter	Nancy Harding	
4 July 1812	Ashburn, Jas.	Sally Davis Taylor	
22 March 1815	Ashburne, Grif.	Lilly Walker	
4 Jan. 1787	Ashburn, Luke	Eliz. Wheeler	
2 May 1837	Ashburn, Wm. G.	Lucy Hughlett	
21 July, 1800	Ashburn, Luke	Susan Roberts	John Roberts father
18 May 1841	Ashburn, Wm.	Sally Walker	
21 Dec. 1802	Ashburn, Geo.	Judith Dodson	
20 July 1823	Atwell, Thos. T.	Dolly J. Palmer	
17 June 1765	Bailey, John	Judith Brent	
8 Jan. 1798	Bailey, Hugh	Frances Chewning spinster	
20 May 1801	Bailey, Hugh	Sally M. Shearman	
21 Apr. 1802	Bailey, Chas.	Mary Chowning Dunaway b. 18 Mch. 1781	Dau. Saml. & Frances Dunaway
18 Oct. 1804	Bailey, Jesse	Lucy Carter	
28 Sept. 1814	Bailey, Chas.	Esther Brown	
25 Nov. 1717	Ball, Saml.	Anne Tayloe	
17 Feb. 1723	Ball, Wm.	Margaret Ball	Dau. Rd. Ball
29 May 1727	Ball, David	Ellen Heale	Dau. Geo. Heale
10 Oct. 1735	Ball, Geo.	Judith Payne	
14 June 1736	Ball, Geo., Jr. of Northumberland	Anna Taylor	Dau. Eliz. Taylor

DATE	GROOM	BRIDE	PARENTS
10 Dec. 1737	Ball, Jesse	Mrs. Frances Burges	Son of Jas. Ball
9 March 1765	Ball, Jesse	Agatha Conway	
12 Mch. 1765	Ball, John	Mary Ball	Dau. of Lettice Ball
30 May 1779	Ball, Jas. W.	Anne Ball	
17 Feb. 1789	Ball, Jesse C.	Peggy Mitchell	
23 Jan. 1797	Ball, Jos. widower	Anne Currell	
8 Apr. 1799	Ball, John S.	Nancy Opie spinster	
12 Apr. 1799	Ball, Spencer	Ann Ball Robertson	Dau. Ann Robertson
3 May 1802	Ball, Joseph	Olivia Chinn	
2 Nov. 1807	Ball, Cyrus	Fidelia Downman	Dau. R. W. Downman
2 Aug. 1819	Ball, Hilkiah	Hannah G. Ball	Dau. Sarah E. Ball
24 Jan. 1822	Ball, John G.	Eliz. T. Payne	Son Jesse Ball, Jno. Payne, Sec.
1 Jan. 1835	Ball, Luke	Rebecca H. Haynie	Dau. Hancock Haynie
15 Nov. 1845	Ball, Hilkiah	Sarah E. Simmons	Thos. Brent, Sec.
13 April 1846	Ball, John B.	Catherine E. Montague	Dau. Lewis B. Montague
16 Dec. 1724	Ballendine, Wm.	Mary Ann Ewel, widow	Thos. Edwards, Sec.
19 Mch. 1802	Bank, Jules E.	Caty Dunaway	
12 Aug. 1724	Bannerman, Mark (of Middlesex Co.)	Catherine Barker	Wm. Payne, Sec.
26 March 1808	Barnett, John	Dolly Sampson	Ezekiel Hayden, Sec.
11 Feb. 1811	Barnett, John	Molly Hayden	Dau. Lucy Hayden
9 July 1836	Barnett, Joseph	Polly George	Jas. Ingram, Sec.
23 Nov. 1813	Barrack, Wm.	Lucy Dunaway	
22 Dec. 1814	Barrack, Newby	Nancy Payne	Dau. Edward Payne
16 Jan. 1821	Barrick, Wm.	Nancy Weymouth	Benj. Walker, Sec.
14 Nov. 1832	Barrick, Griffin	Elizabeth Newby	Rd. Hackney, Sec.

DATE	GROOM	BRIDE	PARENTS, SEC.
4 July 1843	Barrick, Griffin	Eliza B. Stonum	Rd. Coleman, Sec.
22 Oct. 1784	Barrett, Geo.	Ann Haynie	Thos. Pollard, Sec.
20 Dec. 1847	Barrett, Wm. C. of Northumberland	Cephronia George	Robt. S. Dunaway, Sec.
10 Mch. 1764	Bass, John	Mary Degge	Chas. Lee, Sec.
27 Aug. 1793	Basye, Elismond	Betsy Cundiff	John Chilton, Sec.
20 Nov. 1848	Basye, Thos.	M. Eugenie Carter	John B. Branham, Sec.
1 July 1771	Batten, Wm.	Betty Pollard	Thos. Stott, Sec.
13 Aug. 1834	Beacham, Jos.	Sarah Gresham	John Gresham, Sec.
10 July 1764	Beale, Thos. of Richmond Co.	Jane Currie	Dau. David Currie
5 March 1771	Beale, John Eustace	Elizabeth Lee	Dau. Chas. Lee
13 June 1810	Beale, Alford of Richmond Co.	Million Downman	Jos. B. Downman, Sec.
6 Feb. 1839	Beale, Henry	Susan R. Robinson	James Robinson, Sec.
24 Feb. 1844	Beale, Robert	Eliz. N. Robinson	James Robinson, Sec.
16 Nov. 1780	Been, Charles	Judith Edwards	Jno. Been, Sec.
18 Oct. 1788	Bean, George	Polly Warren	Dau. Wm. Warren
5 Nov. 1786	Bean, Peter	Catherine Pollard	
27 Dec. 1790	Bean, Edwin	Eliz. Edwards	
11 Feb. 1811	Bean, John	Molly Hayden	Dau. Lucy Hayden
9 Nov. 1799	Beane, Peter	Betsy Mott	
23 Nov. 1806	Beane, Thos.	Ellen Owen	
19 Jan. 1809	Beane, George	Fanny Sebree	
3 March 1810	Beane, Armistead	Amy Weaver	
25 Oct. 1815	Beane, Peter, Jr.	Eliz. C. Lawson	Dau. Henry Lawson
18 Nov. 1817	Beane, Robt. E.	Mary Biscoe Towell	Dau. Mark Towell
31 Dec. 1823	Beane, John	Armon George	
14 June 1825	Beane, Geo. E.	Eliz. L. Biscoe	
23 Jan. 1826	Beane, John	Cath. Beane	

DATE	GROOM	BRIDE	PARENTS, SEC.
1 Dec. 1828	Beane, Edward	Ann P. Lunsford	
23 Apr. 1831	Beane, Thos. I.	Mary B. Beane	
6 Oct. 1831	Beane, Silas	Milly Cundiff	
18 Nov. 1839	Beane, Warner	Eliz. C. Buchan	Nich. Buchan, Sec.
16 Dec. 1839	Beane, Wm.	Sally Forrester	
13 Feb. 1841	Beane, Rd. T.	Agnes C. Talley	
20 Jan. 1843	Beane, Leroy	Margaret Ann Taff	Son of Francis Beane
21 June 1843	Beane, Wm. I.	Juliet C. Booth	Eliz. F. Booth consent.
13 May 1844	Beane, Peter H.	Frances M. Stott	Richard Hinton, Sec.
1 Jan. 1847	Bee, William	Sealyer, Nickings	
15 July 1748	Bell, John	Franky Edmonds	Wm. Taylor, consent
26 Dec. 1806	Bell, Coleman	Agge Weaver	
10 July 1833	Bell, James, Jr.	Hannah M. Shearman	
28 Oct. 1793	Bennett, Rd. of Westmoreland	Catherine Lawson	(License from Frederick Co.)
16 Jan. 1783	Berry, George	Jane Carter	
5 Dec. 1831	Betts, Royster, Sen.	Catherine Watts	
31 May 1727	Biscoe, Robt.	Eliz. Lawson	Dau. Henry Lawson
2 Dec. 1780	Biscoe, Wm.	Hannah Blakemore	Edw. Blakemore, sec.
13 Feb. 1792	Biscoe, Geo.	Patty Potts	Dau. Thos. Potts
10 Dec. 1804	Biscoe, John	Nancy P. Carpenter	
16 Dec. 1811	Biscoe, John	Jane Carpenter	
7 Sept. 1812	Biscoe, Thos.	Katherine Payne	
18 Dec. 1815	Biscoe Robt.	Nancy Beane	
16 Dec. 1834	Biscoe, Harry L.	Sarah C. Blakemore	
11 Sept. 1747	Blakemore, Edw.	Hannah Stevens of St. Mary's White Chapel	
9 Nov. 1750	Blakemore, Edw.	Jan. Neasum	
8 May 1778	Blakemore, Edw.	Betty Rogers	

Page 5

DATE	GROOM	BRIDE	PARENTS, SEC.
29 Nov. 1801	Blakemore, Wm.	Louisa Chowning	
28 Oct. 1830	Blakemore, Wm.	Lilly T. Thrall	
4 July 1842	Blakey, Robt. L.	Eliz. A. Rogers	
8 June 1811	Bland, Theoderick	Ann Pollard	
28 Nov. 1830	Bland, Francis	Eliz. Hughs	
14 June 1759	Blincoe, John	Mary Connelly	Dau. John Connelly
28 May 1846	Bluefoot, Wm.	Margaret Jones	Dau. Sally Jones
1 July, 1771	Boatman, Wm.	Bridgit Brinin	
18 Jan. 1781	Boatman, Wm.	Sarah Yerby	
19 Jan. 1798	Boatman, John	Nancy Mason	
20 Oct. 1824	Boatman, John	Judith Gundry	
19 Aug. 1833	Boatman, John D.	Marg. C. Perciful	Dau. Margaret Perciful
16 Dec. 1794	Bonawell, Reuben	Grace Wallace	
22 June 1753	Bond, John	Sarah Sharpe	
14 June 1804	Bond, Thos.	Kitty Hill	
26 Dec. 1826	Booth, Wm. P.	Frances Mitchell	
23 June 1846	Boroughs, John of Princess Anne Co.	Eliz. A. Snead	
28 June 1800	Bottoms, Thomas	Hannah Cox b. 21 Feb. 1776	Dau. Thos. Cox
18 Jan. 1841	Bottoms, James	Jane Miller	
28 Dec. 1808	Bowen, James	Nancy Moore	
20 June 1795	Bowles, Benj.	Charlotte Harris	
2 June 1791	Boyd, Robt.	Nancy Pitman	
19 Feb. 1829	Boyd, John	Margaret Dunaway	
1 Jan. 1831	Boyd, Thomas	Eliz. H. George	
20 March 1833	Boyd, David	Leannah Hutchings	
15 July 1833	Boyd, Wm.	Ann Kirkham	Braxton Kirkham
20 Jan. 1799	Booth, Obediah	Frances Davis, widow R. Tapscott	
10 Dec. 1833	Boyd, Thos.	Lucy Wheeler	

DATE	GROOM	BRIDE	PARENTS, SEC.
19 Sept. 1808	Bradberry, Jas.	Peggy Dodson	Dau. Chas. Dodson
6 Dec. 1811	Bradberry, Wm.	Eliz. McTyre	
3 April 1800	Bradley, John	Eliz. Alford	Dau. Robt. & Marg. Alford
21 March 1825	Bradley, William	Dorinda Galloway	Dau. Maria Stimson
25 Apr. 1843	Bradley, William	Caroline Stimson	Dau. Maria Stimson
20 Dec. 1849	Bradley, John	Mary A. Gundry	
14 Mch. 1835	Branham, Jno. B.	Priscila Downman	
19 Oct. 1840	Branham, Jno. B.	Margaret Y. Carter	
16 Jan. 1752/3	Braxton, Geo., Jr.	Mrs. Mary Carter	Dau. Col. Carter of Corotoman
7 Jan. 1723/4	Brent, William	Margaret Haines	
30 Apr. 1926	Brent, Hugh	Eliz. Morris	
26 July 1727	Brent, James	Catherine Martin	
9 Aug. 1735	Brent, Wm.	Letitia Wale	
3 Sept. 1750	Brent, Hugh	Susanna Payne	Dau. Geo. Payne
1 May 1753	Brent, Wm.	Judith King (widow)	
1 Oct. 1761	Brent, Hugh	Easter Shearman	
16 July 1764	Brent, Maurice	Lucy Flower	
4 Oct. 1768	Brent, James	Sarah Cammell	
17 Dec. 1772	Brent, Geo.	Joanna Wale	
20 Oct. 1774	Brent, Thomas	Judith King (widow)	
18 Feb. 1779	Brent, Thomas	Lucy Brent	
14 April 1779	Brent, Newton	Ann Steptoe Lawson	
20 May 1779	Brent, William	Ellinor Stott	
15 Sept. 1779	Brent, Jeduthan	Molly Brent	
25 May 1780	Brent, James	Elizabeth Hunt	
15 Jan. 1784	Brent, Geo.	Sarah Ann Simmons	
24 June 1786	Brent, Vincent	Margaret S. Lawson	
1 Apr. 1791	Brent, John	Judith Norris, widow	
13 Dec. 1791	Brent, Charles (bachelor)	Catherine Kirk (spinster)	Ward of Wm. Kirk

DATE	GROOM	BRIDE	PARENTS, SEC.
8 Feb. 1792	Brent Geo.	Sarah Edmunds	Dau. Elias Edmunds
9 Jan. 1796	Brent, Hugh (widower)	Mary T. Lawson	
12 June 1796	Brent, John	Ann Degges (Spinster)	
20 Dec. 1796	Brent, Martin	Ann Chilton	
17 June 1806	Brent, James	Frances Hunton	
11 Jan. 1809	Brent, Jas. D.	Fanny Brent	
19 Aug. 1809	Brent, William	Elisa Hall	
2 July 1819	Brent, James	Eliz. L. Dameron	
2 July 1821	Brent, James K.	Lucy C. Garlington	
24 Mch. 1814	Brent, James, Jr.	Ann S. Brent	
29 Jan. 1816	Brent, Kenner	Eliz. Brent	
29 Aug. 1816	Brent, Geo., Jr.	Catherine Tapscott	
8 Mch. 1819	Brent, Isaac	Mary Ann Dameron	
20 Nov. 1823	Brent, Wm. H.	Catherine M. Carter	Mary Carter, consent
31 Mch. 1824	Brent, Elias	Eliz. C. Edwards	Bidkar George, gd. Eliz.
21 July 1825	Brent, Chas. S.	Sally McTyre	
15 Jan. 1833	Brent, Rd. W. H.	Sally M. Gibson	
18 Feb. 1834	Brent, James	Mary Wright	
17 Dec. 1825	Bridgeman, Wm.	Jane N. Hunt	John Hunt, consent
17 Feb. 1758	Bristow, James	Agatha Mitchell	
12 Mch. 1783	Bristow, Wm.	Jemima Blakemore	
5 Dec. 1828	Bristow, Larkin S.	Catherine Seward	
24 Oct. 1715	Brockenbrough, N. Rd. Co.	Sarah Neale age 21	
5 Mch. 1726	Brosier, Jos.	Mary Harris	
10 Sept. 1791	Brumly, Daniel	Susanna Holloway age 28	
2 July 1722	Brown, John	Eliz. James	
23 May, 1786	Brown, John	Eliz. Mason	

Page 8

DATE	GROOM	BRIDE	PARENTS, SEC.
24 Jan. 1793	Brown, Wm.	Judith Clayton b. 1766, parents dead 5 yrs.)	
19 Dec. 1796	Wm. Brown, Jr. (widower)	Peggy Hadon (widow)	
20 May 1802	Brown, Spencer	Judith Payne	
17 Jan. 1804	Brown, Wm.	Nancy Hazard	
16 Jan. 1804	Brown, Wm.	Betsy Coats	
20 Feb. 1804	Brown, Wm.	Sally Pitman (widow)	
31 Dec. 1807	Brown, Burges	Molly Mason	
20 Oct. 1807	Brown, Thomas	Eliz. G. Lee	
24 June 1815	Brown, Wm.	Siller G. Stott	
1 Jan. 1817	Brown, Wm.	Susan Coats	
17 Dec. 1817	Brown, Raleigh	Nancy Robinson	
29 Mch. 1829	Brown, Wm.	Catherine Garner	Ward of Thad. Mitchell
8 Apr. 1831	Brown, Wm. W.	Jane T. Hunter	Dau. of Susan Hunter
4 Apr. 1836	Brown, Chas. L.	Maria I. Payne	
13 Dec. 1836	Brown, Jas. W.	Priscilla Kent	
19 July 1837	Brown, Robert	Nancy Dunaway	
19 Dec. 1838	Brown, Vincent	Juliet Ann Connelly	
28 Sept. 1843	Brown, John	Eliz. Robinson	
11 March 1846	Brown, Wash. D.	Mary Susan Walker	
16 Apr. 1846	Brown, Raw. W.	Ann W. George	
27 May 1846	Brown, Ezekiel W.	Eliz. M. R. Janice	
27 Dec. 1821	Brumley, Thos. C.	Polly Hubbard	
7 Jan. 1818	Bryant, John	Margaret S. Dameron	Dau. Thos. Dameron
9 Oct. 1779	Bucher, Wm.	Catherine Hinton	
9 May 1808	Bucher, David	Eliz. H. Currell	Martin Shearman, gdn.
5 Feb. 1816	Bucher, Nicho. P.	Polly Beans	
7 Dec. 1819	Bucher, David	Nancy C. McTyre	Ward of Ailey McTyre
5 Oct. 1721	Burges, Chas.	Frances Fox	Dau. of Ann Fox
20 Apr. 1786	Burwell, Nath.	Frances Wormley	

Page 9

DATE	GROOM	BRIDE	PARENTS
11 Oct. 1720	Bush, Issaac	Hannah Sammon	
8 Mch. 1782	Bush, James	Fanny Jarrett	
30 Oct. 1834	Bush, Thomas	Tomze B. Thomas	
13 Jan. 1846	Bush, James	Frances Stott	
1 Dec. 1794	Callahan, Wm.	Nelly Chowning	
8 Oct. 1817	Callahan, Wm. C.	Betsy Hunt	
15 Apr. 1828	Callahan, Thos. C.	Eliz. R. Blakemore	Son of Wm. Callahan
1 Apr. 1842	Callahan, T. C.	Hannah F. Gresham	
14 Mch. 1723	Cammell, Wm. of Northumberland	Sarah Kelley	
13 Aug. 1756	Cammell, Jas.	Hannah Chilton	
21 Sept. 1787	Campbell, Geo. of Md.	Eliz. Stott	
15 Jan. 1736	Cannaday, John	Catherine Heale	Dau. of Geo. Heale, de
14 Mch. 1723	Carnell, Wm.	Sarah Kelley	
19 June 1809	Causey, James	Polly Smith	
13 Jan. 1717	Carpenter, Thos.	Mary Nichols	
30 June 1746	Carpenter, Nath.	Frances Blackerby	
18 Mch. 1784	Carpenter, John	Ellen Carter	
22 Aug. 1794	Carpenter, Wm.	Sally Bailey	
21 Feb. 1814	Carpenter, W. C.	Harriet Brown	
29 Aug. 1814	Carpenter, Mierome	Lucy Pollard	
2 Apr. 1817	Carpenter, Benj.	Hannah Wiggins	
19 July 1819	Carpenter, Griffin	Margt. C. Newgert	
6 Aug. 1818	Carpenter, W. C.	Molly Stonum	
10 Nov. 1747	Carter, Wm.	Frances Brent	
15 Jan. 1750	Carter, Thos.	Ann Hunter (widow)	
14 June 1751	Carter, Edward	Katherine Brent	
24 July 1753	Carter, Josiah	Betty Dogget	Dau. Wm. Dogget
9 Aug. 1758	Carter, Henry	Hannah Chilton	Ward of Jas. Ball

DATE	GROOM	BRIDE	PARENTS, SEC.
5 Sept. 1765	Carter, Raleigh	Sarah Sharpe	
11 Jan. 1768	Carter, Job	Sarah Rob	Dau. Frances Rob
21 Nov. 1771	Carter Thos.	Eliz. Doggett	
27 July 1778	Carter, Job	Judith Harris	
16 Nov. 1780	Carter, Geo.	Eliz. James	
19 June 1783	Carter, Jos.	Sarah Chilton	
17 Mch. 1785	Carter, John	Peggy Yerby	
16 Feb. 1786	Carter, Edward	Sallie White	
8 Nov. 1786	Carter, John	Martha Dillard	
21 May 1790	Carter, Edward	Judith Lunsford (spinster)	
15 June 1792	Carter, Jos. (bachelor)	Margaret Carter	
22 Jan. 1795	Carter, John, Jr. (widower)	Gracey B. Conway (spinster)	
1 June, 1797	Carter, Jos., Jr.	Fanny E. Hutchings	
18 Nov. 1799	Carter, Thos.	Judith Palmer	
17 Feb. 1807	Carter, Martin	Sally Craine	
21 Sept. 1807	Carter, James, Jr.	------------	
22 Nov. 1815	Carter, Hump. F.	Frances Ravenscroft Ball	Dau. Jas. Ball
24 Dec. 1816	Carter, John	Mrs. Carmen Pullen	
28 Oct. 1817	Carter, Jos. A.	Eliza C. Nutt	
18 Feb. 1818	Carter, Hiram	Emily Tankersley	
16 Apr. 1821	Carter, John	Mary Ann G. Hammonds	
31 Jan. 1822	Carter, Edward	Frances Kent	
15 Dec. 1824	Carter, Dale	Sally B. Oldham	
19 Apr. 1830	Carter, Ralph	Sally B. Oldham	
23 Feb. 1832	Carter, Wm. H.	Harriet Ball	Ward of R. Pinckard
2 Jan. 1841	Carter, Addis. L.	Mary D. Jones	Letter from Eliza C. Jones

DATE	GROOM	BRIDE	PARENTS, SEC.
23 Aug. 1785	Cary, John of Gloucester Co.	Eliz. Williams	
16 Feb. 1786	Carter, Martin	Milly Dunaway	
11 July 1729	Chichester, Rd.	Ann Fox, widow of Wm. Fox	
3 July 1734	Chichester, Rd.	Ellen Ball	Dau. of Wm. Ball
7 June 1759	Chichester, Rd.	Ann Gordon	Dau. James Gordon
30 Dec. 1795	Chichester, D. P.	Catherine Sydnor	
14 Jan. 1723/4	Chilton, Thos.	Winifred King	Dau. of Elesbee Pasquet
19 Nov. 1767	Chiltom, Jesse	Ann Smith	
22 Aug. 1783	Chilton, Newman or Shelton	Eliz. Edmonds	
27 Dec. 1783	Chilton, Henry	Ann Flowers	
23 Dec. 1788	Chilton, Andrew	Eliz. Davis	
7 Nov. 1796	Chitton, Jesse	Nancy Galloway	
18 June 1804	Chitton, Cyrus	Leanna Beane	
24 Nov. 1804	Chitton, Edwin	Betsy Chitten	
8 Feb. 1804	Chitton, Merryman	Hannah Rogers	
1 Apr. 1817	Chitton, Stephen	Harriet Doggett	
26 Nov. 1818	Chitton, Hiram	Polly Yopp	
25 Jan. 1819	Chilton, Newman	Lucinda Spilman	
29 Dec. 1824	Chilton, Griffin	Eliz. T. Kirk	Ward of Kemar Brent
23 July 1827	Chilton, Rd.	Betsy Keeling	
24 Nov. 1828	Chilton, Faunt. V.	Sally G. Mitchell	
19 Jan. 1829	Chilton, R. N.	Anna C. Chewning	
20 May 1844	Chilton, Jesse G.	Sally R. George	Dau. Jesse George
8 Nov. 1845	Chilton, Jno. R.	Anna C. Chilton	
2 May 1727	Chinn, Jos.	Mrs. Eliz. Ball	

Page 12

DATE	GROOM	BRIDE	PARENTS, SEC.
12 Nov. 1735	Chinn, Thomas	Sarah Mitchell	
26 Oct. 1739	Chinn, Chichester	Agatha Thornton	Son of Raleigh Chinn
11 July 1752	Chinn, Thos.	Mrs. Annie Edmonds	
16 Oct. 1764	Chinn, Thos., Jr. (widower)	Sarah Brent	
8 Feb. 1797	Chinn, Rawleigh (bachelor)	Eliz. Shearman (spinster)	
8 June 1799	Chinn, Bartho.	Olivia Downman	Dau. J. B. Downman
21 July 1828	Chinn, Barth. C.	Millian E. Downman	
18 May 1780	Chitwood, Wm.	Betty Neale	
21 Oct. 1822	Chitwood, Wm.	Lucy Pitman	
20 Dec. 1827	Chitwood, Wm.	Nancy Thrift	
9 Jan. 1845	Chitwood, Wm.	Mary Jane Barnes	
28 Dec. 1764	Chowning, Wm. of Middlesex	Thomasin Sharpe	
24 Aug. 1769	Chowning, Henry	Eunice Bailey	
18 Nov. 1839	Chowning, Leroy	Cordelia Oldham	
28 Nov. 1840	Chowning, Jno. S.	Mary M. K. Mitchell	
6 July 1756	Christian, Francis	Katherine Chinn	Dau. of Ann Chinn
22 Oct. 1761	Christian, Chris.	Judah Davis of age	
16 Dec. 1769	Christian, Francis	Ann Shearman	Dau. of M. & Ann Shearman
27 Dec. 1788	Christian, Chris.	Easter Newsom	
19 July 1781	Christopher, John	Dolly Fleet	
18 Mch. 1808	Christopher, Thos.	Achsah Dunaway	
16 Dec. 1833	Christopher, J. H.	Eliz. Robinson	
26 Oct. 1839	Christopher, Geo.	Amelia T. Parker	
17 Aug. 1801	Church, Wm.	Betsy J. Davis	
12 Jan. 1809	Church, Wm. of Middlesex	Ellen Gundry	

Page 13

DATE	GROOM	BRIDE	PARENT, SEC.
23 Sept. 1762	Churchill, Wm.	Eliz. Edwards	
16 May 1756	Clark, Daniel	Anney Shelton	
15 May 1786	Clark, Jesse	Eliz. Miller	
25 May 1786	Clarke, Robt.	Judith Wilkerson	
7 Nov. 1795	Clarke, Gardner	Judith Beane	
7 July 1832	Clarke, Wm. T.	Nancy Connelly	
4 June 1838	Clarke, J. L.	Eliz. Oldham	
3 Oct. 1838	Clarke, Humph.	Ann Kent	
7 June 1843	Clarke, Wm.	Ann Clarke	
17 Mch. 1845	Clark, Benj. D.	Octavia A. Ball	
7 May 1850	Clarke, Thos. R.	Jane Doggett	
11 May 1786	Coates, Raw.	Catherine Die	
12 Jan. 1800	Coats, Rawl.	Mrs. Sarah Weiblin (widow)	
2 Nov. 1813	Coates, Rd.	Molly Garner	
3 Aug. 1816	Coates, Thos.	Molly Coates	
18 Nov. 1822	Coates, Thos.	Sally Watts	
29 July 1834	Coats, Thos of Northumberland	Polly Seebry (widow)	
26 Mch. 1728	Cockerell, Presly	Susannah Whaley	
12 May 1812	Cockerell, Rd.	Nancy Sampson	
29 Nov. 1822	Coleman, Rd.	Eliz. Barrick	Dau. Reuben Barrick
17 June 1833	Coleman, Rd.	Mildred Palmer	T. G. Atwell, gd.
7 Sept. 1850	Coleman, Jas. H.	Tomza Callahan	
19 June 1821	Coles, Rd. P.	Anaianda Myers	
16 Apr. 1772	Connelly, Patrick	Ann Doggett	
29 Nov. 1798	Connelly, Patrick	Lucy Connally	

DATE	GROOM	BRIDE	PARENTS
23 Apr. 1778	Connelly, John	Mary Stephens 21 next June	
26 Dec. 1792	Conally, Wm.	Margaret Hill	
18 Mch. 1816	Connally, Wmson.	Nancy Rogers	
17 Dec. 1825	Connelly, Jas.	Mary Smith	
16 Dec. 1833	Conelly, Wm.	Judith C. Hazzard	
16 Sept. 1844	Conoly, Wm. S.	Noary L. Cockrell	
8 Apr. 1843	Coppedge, Cyrus T.	Mary E. Hutchings	
24 May 1811	Corbin, Gawin	Nancy Meredith	
8 Dec. 1817	Corbin, Geo. L.	Sarah D. Spriggs	
20 Dec. 1790	Cornelius, Wm.	---------	John Lawson, Sec.
May 22, 1790	Cornelius, Thos.	Eliz. Dameron	Dau. Aaron Dameron
May 10, 1808	Cornelius, John	Eliz. Robins	
May 5, 1819	Cornelius, James	Sally James	
May 11, 1824	Cornelius, West	Sarah Cornelius	
Dec. 31, 1831	Cornelius, Bailey	Milly Barnett	
Nov. 19, 1838	Cornelius, John	Judith Hammond	
Jan. 7, 1841	Cornelius, Jas. C.	Anna Walker	
Feb. 14, 1844	Cornelius, Wm. B.	Mahala Longworth	
Feb. 2, 1805	Cornish, Geo. D.	Jenny Perciful	
Oct. 28, 1833	Costello, John	Sally Lee Lunsford	
Oct. 22, 1788	Cotterell, Wm. (Northumberland)	Judith Gibbs	
Jan. 17, 1799	Cottrell, Thos.	Betsy Thomas	
Nov. 30, 1843	Connellee, Jos.	Sophronia Ayres	Dau. of Jno. Ayres
Feb. 3, 1840	Covington, Thos. D.	Ann Eliza Taylor	
Sept. 19, 1803	Cowles, Wm. T.	Sarah Spriggs	
Oct. 17, 1723	Cox, Presley	Mary Fleet	Dau. of Henry Fleet
June 15, 1789	Cox, John	Mary Whealer	

DATE	GROOM	BRIDE	PARENTS
June 16, 1790	Cox, Thos.	Jemima Kent, widow	
Jan. 17, 1814	Cox, John	Cretia Kent	
July 16, 1821	Cox, Fleet	Elizabeth Kent	
21 Mch. 1827	Cox, Presley W.	Martha A. Ingram	
4 Jan. 1837	Cox, Presley	Sarah Locke	
27 Oct. 1842	Cox, James	Roxy Pinn	
15 Oct. 1845	Cox, Jesse	Eliz. Tankersley	
24 Aug. 1787	Craine, Isaac	Sally Sullivant (Married Aug. 29)	
24 Jan. 1799	Creath, Jacob	Milly V. Carter	
9 June 1763	Creswell, Jas.	Mary Garlington	
11 July 1787	Criswell, Jas.	Judith M. Conway	
8 Nov. 1830	Crutcher, Rd.	Amanda Brown	
21 Sept. 1836	Crittenden, Zach.	Mary F. Edmonds	
7 Dec. 1840	Crittenden, G. W.	Susan C. Hall	
5 Sept. 1809	Crom, Andrew	Alice Pinckard	Dau. Eliz. Pinckard
20 May 1812	Crowder, Thos.	Eliz. H. Currell	
3 Sept. 1835	Crowder, John	Eliz. S. Kent	
16 Mch. 1843	Crum, Jos.	Cathan Tomas	
6 Aug. 1742	Crump, Adam of Prince Wm. Co.	Hannah Heale, wid.	
2 Feb. 1788	Cundiff, Rd.	Ellen Forester	
20 July 1791	Cundiff, John	Fanny Pinckard	
13 Oct. 1795	Cundiff, Benj.	Alcey F. McTyre	
19 Sept. 1796	Cundiff, Wm.	Catherine Sullivant (widow)	
20 Jan. 1824	Cundiff, John	Ruth Nutt	
7 Dec. 1825	Cundiff, Isaac	Polly Basye	
1 Dec. 1828	Cundiff, Isaac	Pamela Carter	
7 Apr. 1758	Curd, John of Goochland	Lucy Brent	

Page 16

DATE	GROOM	BRIDE	PARENT
10 July 1750	Currell, Nich.	Margaret Lawson	
22 July 1750	Currell, Harry	Amy Hains	
31 Dec. 1757	Currell, Spencer	Judith Bridgford	
6 Jan. 1772	Currell, Isaac	Dolly Hathaway	
20 May 1779	Currell, Jas. Jr.	Frances James	
15 Apr. 1794	Currell, Rawl.	Judith Cox	Dau. of Thos. Cox.
16 Nov. 1790	Currell, Fleet	Sarah C. Reaves	
20 Mch. 1787	Currell, Robt.	Mary King	
24 July 1790	Currell, Jacob	Lucy Schofield	Letter from Jacob says Lucy has no parent
17 June 1793	Currell, Spencer	Lucy Hinton	Dau. Cath. Buchan
8 Dec. 1796	Currell, Fleet (bachelor)	Mary James (spinster)	
10 Apr. 1798	Currell, Edward	Eliz. Sydnor	
17 Dec. 1801	Currell, Thos.	Mary George	
17 July 1815	Currell, Jake	Sally Currell	
17 July 1815	Currell, Isaac	Mrs. Polly S. Kemm	
14 July 1829	Currell, Wm.	Lucy Kemm	Ward of Elias Brent
6 May 1830	Currell, Isaac	Mary S. George	
12 Jan. 1831	Currell, Wm.	Eliz. James	
24 Apr. 1843	Currell, Wm. C.	Frances M. George	
20 Dec. 1848	Currell, John Y.	Emily M. Mitchell	
12 Mch. 1808	Currie, Armist.	Jane M. Gilliam	
7 June 1810	Currie, Armistead	Mary B. Jones	Dau. Gawin Corbin
13 Mch. 1847	Currie, A. H.	Cordelia C. Chowning	
17 May 1771	Curtis, Hillary	Betty Doggett (spinster)	
12 May 1789	Curtice, Thos.	Betsy Chilton	
21 Nov. 1789	Curtice, Chas.	Anne George (of age)	Dau. Spencer George
18 Oct. 1797	Curtis, Nich.	Sarah Dameron (widow)	
15 May 1790	Cuthbert, Wm.	Ann Lawson (widow)	

Page 17

DATE	GROOM	BRIDE	PARENTS
12 Sept. 1728	Dameron, John of Northumberland Co.	Elizabeth Taylor	
26 Apr. 1794	Dameron, Thos.	Sally Brown (b. 29 Sept. 1767)	
26 Sept. 1794	Dameron, John	Molly Brown	Dau. Elias Brown
17 July 1798	Dameron, Samuel	Lucy Potts	
16 Jan. 1799	Dameron, Thos.	Sally W. Roberts	Dau. Jno. & Eliz. Roberts
30 Apr. 1800	Dameron, Holland	Betsy Williams	
20 Feb. 1802	Dameron, G. W.	Ann H. Steel (of age)	
9 Dec. 1816	Dameron, Dennis	Eliz. Haydon	Dau. of Wm. O. Haydon
31 Jan. 1834	Dameron, Wm.	Judith Gaskins	
4 June, 1785	Dance, Thos.	Sally Hinton	
9 Mch. 1825	Dandridge, W. H.	Maria L. Jones	
22 Aug. 1797	Daniel, Robt.	Hannah Rogers	
13 Mch. 1803	Daniel, Beverley	Judith B. Bailey	
8 Feb. 1806	Daniel, Garrett	Sally Riveer	
20 June 1809	Dawson, Wm.	Judith Jones Moore	
31 Oct. 1831	Dawson, Wm.	Frances A. Tarkelson	
7 Feb. 1839	Dawson, John	Ann Thrall	
14 Mch. 1839	Darity, Wm.	Matilda P. Hill	
8 Mch. 1784	Davenport, Geo.	June Harris	
15 Dec. 1806	Davenport, D. D.	Sarah F. Hudnall	
9 Dec. 1817	Davenport, J. P.	Lucy Simmons	
10 May 1834	Davenport, Fort. of Richmond Co.	Adeline Latham	
1 Jan. 1838	Davenport, Rd. O.	Lucy G. Hubbard	
30 Dec. 1766	Davis, John, Jr.	Caty McTyre	Dau. Robt. McTyre
1 Jan. 1779	Davis, Geo.	Frances White	
23 Jan. 1787	Davis, Richard	Mary Crowder	Married Feb. 2.
5 Feb. 1791	Davis, Jos.	Susannah Church	Dau. Samuel Church

Page 18

DATE	GROOM	BRIDE	PARENTS
4 Dec. 1794	Davis, Jos.	Winifred Warnick	
11 May 1799	Davis, Bartley	Nancy Dodson	
7 Feb. 1805	Davis, Capt. Rd.	Elizabeth Brown	
14 Feb. 1815	Davis, Richard	Sarah Chilton Dye	
16 Oct. 1816	Davis, Robert	Polly C. Perciful	
9 Apr. 1828	Davis, Jesse	Eliz. S. B. Barnet	
21 Mch. 1839	Davis, Wm.	Mary Chilton	
2 Jan. 1843	Davis, Thos.	Patsy Fleming	
7 Feb. 1850	Davis, Thos.	Keturah F. Beane	
19 Feb. 1828	Dawson, Wm. H.	Maria Kirkham	
13 Oct. 1831	Dawson, Wm.	Ann Thomas	Dau. Susan Thomas
22 Dec. 1803	Day, Robert	Kitty Hill	
17 Feb. 1825	Day, William	Delia Lewin	
6 Dec. 1807	Dedford, John	Judith M. George	
1 Mch. 1760	Deforest, Cornelius	Sarah Muse	
4 Sept. 1788	Degge, Wm. of Gloucester Co.	Mary Kirk	
21 July 1794	Degges, Wm. of Mathews Co.	Catherine King	
1 Dec. 1801	Degges, John	Sarah Hathaway	
17 July 1809	Degge, John T.	Polly Brent	
2 Dec. 1834	Degges, Jas. B.	Eliza Ann Towill	
22 Oct. 1835	Degges, W. C.	Amelia A. Degges	
6 Dec. 1836	Denny, John	Roxy H. Lunsford	
17 Jan. 1842	Dewbre, Robt.	Josephine T. Jasper	
7 May 1735	Dickie, Adam Clk. Drysdale Psh.	Ann Thacker	
17 May 1841	Dies, Hiram I.	Matilda P. Daugherty	
21 July 1794	Diggs, Wm. of Mathews Co.	Catherine King	
17 June 1761	Dillard, John	Hannah McTyre	Dau. Robt. McTyre

DATE	GROOM	BRIDE	PARENT
30 Oct. 1841	Dines, Tyson	Mary S. Stokes	
16 Feb. 1841	Dix, Lewis H.	Mary A. Tapscott	Dau. Robt. Tapscott
10 Feb. 1845	Dix, Lewis H.	Kitty Ann Brownley	
22 Aug. 1786	Dobbs, Jos.	Mary Schofield Married Aug. 24.	
11 Dec. 1809	Dobyns, Chris.	Lucy Chowning	
23 Dec. 1841	Dobyns, Joseph	Margaret Travis	Dau. of Ellen Travis
8 Nov. 1843	Dobyns, Edwin L.	Catherine Kirkmyer	
30 June 1803	Dodson, Wm.	Sabra Sullivant	
13 Feb. 1821	Dodson, Rd.	Eliz. G. George	
1 Jan. 1825	Dodson, Alex.	Nancy Cotterall	
25 May 1850	Doll, Penfield	Jane E. Mitchell	
21 Jan. 1779	Doggett, Elmore	Mary Ann Hammonds	
3 Aug. 1779	Doggett, Wm.	Maryann Doggett	
16 June 1785	Doggett, Wm.	Sarah George	
15 Sept. 1785	Doggett, Wm.	Judith Robb	
30 Mch. 1786	Doggett, Elmour	Eliz. Roberts	
18 Sept. 1787	Doggett, Wm. "the younger"	Catherine Dunaway (widow)	
1 Nov. 1791	Doggett, Wm. C.	Nancy B. Cox	Dau. Thos. Cox
19 Dec. 1791	Doggett, Benj.	Eliz. Stott (spinster)	
19 Jan. 1795	Doggett, Geo.	Judith Davis	
17 Aug. 1795	Doggett, John, Jr.	Judith Longworth	
10 Dec. 1795	Doggett, James	Betsy Doggett	
26 Oct. 1798	Doggett, Coleman	Mary Ann Hutchings	
18 July 1803	Doggett, Dennis	Nancy D. Webb	
15 Apr. 1805	Doggett, James	Sarah Doggett	
31 Mch. 1808	Doggett, J. Griggs	Seillah Palmer	
20 Dec. 1810	Doggett, Griffin	Polly Hill	
12 Dec. 1819	Doggett, Samuel	Lucinda Wood Chilton	

DATE	GROOM	BRIDE	PARENT
20 Dec. 1819	Doggett, Wm. S.	Charlotte T. Beane	
16 Oct. 1820	Doggett, Benj.	Nancy P. Barrick	
20 Dec. 1830	Doggett, Thos.	Sarah Pitman	
14 Mch. 1833	Doggett, Wm.	Catherine Pitman	
3 Jan. 1849	Doggett, Wm.	Pamela Hathaway	
16 Aug. 1849	Doggett, Robert	Frances Barrick	
16 Aug. 1806	Donnell, Garrott	Sally Riveer	
29 July 1824	Douglas, Edw.	Eliza Bailey	
16 Dec. 1841	Douglas, Rd.	Frances A. Reade	
21 Feb. 1772	Dove, James	Nancy Fleming	
22 Oct. 1765	Downing, Sam.	Mary Robertson	
4 Oct. 1796	Downing, Edw.	Hannah Ball	
29 Mch. 1836	Downing, Sam., Jr.	Catherine E. Payne	
12 June 1747	Downman, Wm.	Mrs. Ellen Chichester (widow)	
28 Dec. 1764	Downman, Trav. of Northumberland Co.	Anne Conway, widow	
25 May 1783	Downman, Rawl. W.	Priscilla Chinn	
14 Oct. 1811	Downman, Jos. B.	Priscilla Downman	Dau. R. W. Downman
28 Mch. 1814	Downman, Raw. W. of Richmond Co.	Cordelia Gilmour	
18 Dec. 1816	Downman, Wm.	Susan Hudnall	
6 Jan. 1816	Downman, Jno. B.	Harriet J. Downman	
16 Aug. 1830	Downman, Ral. W.	Eliz. F. Currie	
1 Jan. 1808	Dozier, Rd. T.	Nelly Norris	
21 Mch. 1814	Dozier, Thos.	Huldy Hammond	
4 May 1841	Dozier, Thos.	Eliz. D. Hazzard	
9 June 1812	Driver, Wm.	Aley Hammond	
18 Dec. 1779	Dunnaway, Sam.	Ann Davenport	
14 Dec. 1791	Dunnaway, Chatwin	Milly Hill	
16 Oct. 1797	Dunnaway, Geo. C.	Eliz. Norris	

Page 21

DATE	GROOM	BRIDE	PARENTS
6 Jan. 1801	Dunnaway, Thos.	Janny Reveer	
2 Sept. 1802	Dunnaway, Opie	Winny James Palmer	
16 Dec. 1802	Dunnaway, Sam.	Sally Seurlock	
21 Apr. 1812	Dunnaway, Jos.	Nancy Winder	
22 Aug. 1815	Dunnaway, Chatwin	Eliz. Chilton	
6 July 1816	Dunnaway, Jos.	Nancy Angle	
27 Apr. 1818	Dunaway, Rawl.	Frances E. Carter	
19 Nov. 1824	Dunnaway, Capt. T. L.	Felicia T. Hall	
16 Dec. 1828	Dunaway, R. T.	Frances Simmonds	
22 Jan. 1831	Dunaway, Sam.	Winifred Umphries	
20 Jan. 1834	Dunaway, U. B.	Frances M. Carter	
9 Dec. 1835	Dunaway, Isaac	Eliza Dunaway	
12 Dec. 1835	Dunaway, Henry	Polly Talley	
25 Sept. 1837	Dunaway, R. T.	Mary D. George	
1 Jan. 1840	Dunaway, Henry	Eliz. Talley	
18 Oct. 1841	Dunaway, Rawl., Sr.	Anne C. George	
28 Apr. 1842	Dunaway, Epa. N.	Eliz. T. Hathaway	
25 Dec. 1843	Dunaway, Jas. M.	Ann C. Chilton	
20 Feb. 1850	Dunaway, T. S.	Ann Maria Walker	
21 July 1793	Duncan, David	Nancy Branham Demeritt	Dau. Jno. Demeritt
8 Apr. 1794	Dunton, Wm.	Sarah George b. 26 Feb. 1773	Dau. Benj. & Cath. George
15 July 1799	Dunton, Daniel	Milly George	
20 May 1820	Dunton, Wm.	Judith Hathaway	
4 Oct. 1837	Dunton, Wm.	Eliz. Hayden	
16 Sept. 1773	Dye, John	Sally Day	
5 Mch. 1789	Dye, John	Judith Chilton	
17 Aug. 1787	Eaton, Elijah	Dorothy Davis	
10 June 1769	Edmonds, Robt.	Anne Conway	
19 June 1762	Edmonds, Robt.	Eliz. Lee Taylor	
24 Mch 1809	Edmonds, Ralph	Grace Spiller	

Page 22

DATE	GROOM	BRIDE	PARENT
20 Apr. 1812	Edmonds, John	Jane W. Kent	
1 Jan. 1817	Edmonds, Ralph	Frances B. Hall	Dau. John Hall
5 Apr. 1826	Edmonds, John	Nancy Bland	
6 Mch. 1827	Edmonds, Ralph	Mary Ann Eustace	Ward of John Payne
11 Dec. 1828	Edmonds, J. W. A.	Ann Y. Kirk	
3 Jan. 1832	Edmonds, T. W.	Ailcey D. Beale	
13 Dec. 1837	Edmonds, Elias B.	Matilda Jane Payne	
15 Jan. 1838	Edmonds, Robt.	Elizabeth George	Dau. Zamoth George
1 Apr. 1850	Edmonds, F. B.	Jane W. K. Edmunds	
4 Aug. 1772	Edwards, Thos.	Sarah Swan	
6 July 1730	Edwards, Wm.	Eliz. Griggs	Dau. Mrs. Frances Wells
13 July 1736	Edwards, Dr. John of Gloucester Co.	Ann Swan	
20 Feb. 1750	Edwards, Robt.	Ann Chinn	
18 Mch. 1773	Edwards, Wm.	Franky Carter	Dau. Dale Carter
14 Sept. 1775	Edwards, Chas.	Sarah Meredith	Dau. Jno. Meredith
7 Mch. 1797	Edwards, Chas. (widower)	Sally See (spinster)	
12 Dec. 1806	Edwards, Edw.	Eliz. Lewis Foddery	
28 Jan. 1807	Edwards, Wm.	Jency Swanson	
27 Oct. 1814	Edwards, John, Jr.	Margaret Towles	
2 June 1825	Edwards, Grif.	Betsy Ledford	Dau. of Jno. Ledford
28 July 1825	Edwards, David	Florinda F. Thatcher	
1 Mch. 1832	Edwards, Elias	Sophia Edwards	
17 May 1849	Edwards, Wm. B.	Maria Hall	
16 Dec. 1793	Edgar, Samuel	Hannah Steptoe age 21	Dau. Mrs. Joanna Hutchings
16 Sept. 1779	Ellett, Thos.	Sarah Lee	
17 June 1779	Elliott, Alex.	Judith Davis	
7 Aug. 1821	Elliott, Robt.	Sally Davis	

Page 23

DATE	GROOM	BRIDE	PARENT
31 Dec. 1814	England, Geo.	Martha Conway Taylor	
12 Jan. 1815	England, Geo.	Matilda Wesley Waddy	
18 Mch. 1802	Eubank, Giles	Caty Dunaway	
11 Jan. 1842	Eubank, Warner	Fanny B. Edmonds	Dau. Ralph Edmonds
15 Apr. 1757	Eustace, Isaac	Agatha Conway	
24 June 1806	Eustace, John	Maria Leland	Baldwin Leland, Gd.
23 Aug. 1833	Eustace, Jno. H.	Margaret E. Payne	
17 May 1849	Eustace, Wm. B.	Maria Hall	
19 Feb. 1789	Evans, Thos.	Dorcas Cornelius	
3 May 1819	Evans, Robt.	Alcy T. Carter	
11 Jan. 1847	Evans, Jos.	Charlotte Garner	Dau. Griffin Garner
10 Jan. 1795	Everitt, J. D.	Martha Berryman	
1 Jan. 1800	Everitt, J. D.	Alice G. Harrison	
27 Sept. 1736	Ewell, Chas.	Sarah Ball	
10 Jan. 1746	Ewell, Sol.	Eve Taylor (widow)	
18 Dec. 1762	Ewell, Jas.	Sarah Ann Conway	
20 Nov. 1784	Ewell, Jas.	Margaret Robertson	
7 July 1836	Ewell, Jas.	Mira A. Chowning	
10 Jan. 1805	Fallin, Wm.	Nancy Norris, Jun.	
27 Dec. 1736	Fauntleroy, M. of Northumberland	Ann Heale	Son of Wm. Fauntleroy
2 Apr. 1791	Fauntleroy, Robt.	Sarah Ball	
21 May 1762	Fendla, Geo.	Frances Carter	
15 Aug. 1787	Fendla, John	Sally Lee Schofield	
24 Nov. 1815	Fendla, Elias	Winna C. Hayden	
1 June 1835	Fendla, Elias	Harriett George	
5 May 1836	Fendla, Elias	Lucy Bottoms	
31 Feb. 1819	Fendla, James	Janetta Carter	
24 Feb. 1789	Fendla, Thos.	Nancy Jones	

DATE	GROOM	BRIDE	PARENTS
3 Feb. 1781	Ficklin, Jos.	Easter Newby	
25 July 1786	Filk, Amos	Peggy Mason	
20 Mch. 1837	Fitzhugh, Henry of Culpeper Co.	Jane E. Downman	
28 July 1730	Fitzhugh, Henry, Jr. of Stafford Co.	Lucy Carter	
1 Nov. 1718	Fleet, Wm.	Ann Jones	
29 May 1746	Fleet, John of Christ Ch.	Mary Edwards	
31 Jan. 1800	Fleming, Wm.	Sally Mason	
11 Jan. 1746	Flint, Thos.	Hannah Blackmore	
30 Aug. 1797	Flint, Thos.	Priscilla Newby	
16 Mch. 1801	Flowers, John, Jr.	Sally Carter	
27 May 1773	Ford, Capt. Danl.	Eliz. W. Currell	Dau. of Harry Currell
7 Jan. 1809	Ford, Thos. N.	Frances H. George	
15 July 1715	Forrester, Wm. of Richmond Co.	Frances Bryant	Thos. Bryant, father
24 July 1838	Forrester, Thad.	Patsy B. Doggett	
21 Feb. 1821	Foster, Joshua	Sarah D. Allen	
12 Aug. 1777	Ford, Capt. Geo.	Mary Lawson	
15 Dec. 1818	Francis, Wm.	Chloe Ingram	Dau. of Mary Ingram
14 June 1791	Frazier, John	Mary Thomas (widow)	
12 Mch. 1833	Frust, Alex.	Sally George	
31 July 1797	Fullington, Alex.	Lucy Walker	
26 June 1722	Galbraith, Capt. Robt. of Middlesex	Margaret Carter (widow)	
27 Dec. 1786	Gallaway, Jas.	Nancy Wright	
13 Apr. 1799	Galloway, Kemp	Sukey Wallace	
19 Dec. 1812	Galloway, Jas. B.	Ann F. Smither	
30 June 1808	Galloway, Kemp	Sarah Snow (widow)	Widow of Spencer Snow
7 Oct. 1799	Galle, Severe	Alcey F. Conway	
3 Jan. 1816	Ganes, John	Polly Waymouth	
16 Mch. 1791	Garland, Griffin (widower)	Frances Burwell (widow)	

Page 25

DATE	GROOM	BRIDE	PARENTS
5 May 1724	Garlington, Chris.	Eliz. Conway	
8 Nov. 1777	Garlington, Wm.	Lucy Currell	Dau. Geo. Currell
25 Nov. 1782	Garner, Wm.	Ellen Mercer	
24 Mch. 1802	Garner, Wm.	Charlotte McTyre	Dau. Fanny McTyre
27 Feb. 1811	Garner, Thos.	Molly Coates	
27 Dec. 1816	Garner, Wm.	Kitty Shilton	
23 July 1823	Garner, Wm.	Susan Brown	
20 July 1830	Garner, Wm.	Lucy Bailey	
16 Dec. 1839	Garner, Wm., Jr.	Sarah Ann Bailey	
17 June 1846	Garner, Wm.	Sarah D. Berrick	
26 Mch. 1830	Garrett, Wm.	Margaret Brown	
20 Apr. 1786	Ganton, Anthony	Lettice Wheeler	
19 Apr. 1819	Garton, Samuel	Polly Marling	
23 Feb. 1842	Garton, Benj.	Mary Marsh	
31 Dec. 1805	Gaskins, Jos.	Sally Gaskins	
11 Feb. 1842	Gaskins, Edw. W.	Eliz. H. Yerby	
11 Nov. 1845	Gaskins, Edw.	Eliza Swanson	
19 Jan. 1789	Ganton, Benj.	Molly Reeves	
10 June 1762	George, Nich.	Frances Connelly	
19 Oct. 1780	George, Jeduth.	Danas Tapscott	
2 Dec. 1782	George, Wm.	Molly Mercer	
17 Apr. 1783	George, Nich. Lawson	Susanna Tapscott	
2 July 1785	George, Wm.	Eliza Linton Arms	
16 Mch. 1786	George, Zamoth	Fanny Pearson	
20 Oct. 1786	George, Fortun.	Judith Norris	
15 Feb. 1790	George, Tarpley	Eliz. James	
18 Aug. 1794	George, Wm. (long)	Barbara Dobyns	
21 Nov. 1796	George, Spencer, Jr.	Susanna Brent	

Page 26

DATE	GROOM	BRIDE	PARENTS
29 Nov. 1796	George, Wm.(widower)	Sarah Wilder	
21 Mch. 1797	George, Bailey	Nancy George	
21 Aug. 1801	George, Wm.	Polly Chilton	
20 May 1802	George, Moses	Alley Mason	
31 Jan. 1803	George, Wm.	Nancy Angel	
8 Apr. 1806	George, Zamoth	Mary K. James	
10 Apr. 1805	George, Wm.	Behethland N. Payne	
20 Sept. 1808	George, Enoch	Alice Martin Garland	Dau. of Frances Garland
14 Oct. 1808	George, Isaac	Winney Brown	Dau. Spencer Brown
5 May 1812	George, Capt. B.	Mary Degge	
15 Apr. 1815	George, Spencer	Sarah E. Miller	
3 July 1815	George, Moses	Molly Chilton	
6 Jan. 1816	George, Wm. (S.D.)	Jane Hathaway	
27 Sept. 1816	George, Lawson	Judith Palmer	
11 Dec. 1816	George, Enoch	Nancy Julia Myers	Dau. Thos. Myers
2 Jan. 1817	George, Benj.	Judith Doggett	
6 Mch. 1817	George, William	Fanny Pullen	
24 Sept. 1817	George, Lawson	Lucy Tapscott	
16 Dec. 1818	George, Zamoth	Nancy C. Currell	
1 Jan. 1822	George, Wickliff	Mary Towles	
9 Feb. 1822	George, Jesse	Judith Lunsford	
9 July 1822	George, Spencer	Mary Pitman	
15 Jan. 1822	George, Mich. W.	Judith M. Shelton	
21 Jan. 1823	George, Martin	Rebecca M. Stott	
19 May 1823	George, Thos. N.	Harriett Hayden	
3 May 1824	George, Jas. B.	Mary Ruby Flint	
2 June 1824	George, Tarpley	Sarah Ann Wilder	
11 Nov. 1824	George, Wm. H.	Judith Sampson	

Page 27

DATE	GROOM	BRIDE	PARENTS
13 Nov. 1826	George, Spencer	Pauline Lawson	Dau. H. C. Lawson
11 Jan. 1827	George, T. Dobins	Ann K. Patrick	
17 Jan. 1827	George, Monroe	Ann Lunsford	
24 Dec. 1827	George, Mich. W.	Elizabeth Jefferson	
19 Feb. 1828	George, Martin	Jane M. Williams	
23 July 1830	George, Bidkar	Matilda C. Dobyns	
21 Dec. 1830	George, John M.	Ann C. Thrall	
19 Dec. 1831	George, Benj. G.	Catherine L. George	Betsy George mother of bride
11 Nov. 1833	George, Harrison C.	Dorothy S. Carter	
26 Dec. 1834	George, Newton	Ann Mealy	
21 Dec. 1835	George, Leonard	Mariah R. Proper	
17 Aug. 1836	George, Mich. W.	Judith D. George	
29 Sept. 1836	George, War. W.C.	Eliz. Palmer	Dau. Sally Palmer
14 Feb. 1837	George, Benj.	Dorinda Ingram	
26 Feb. 1837	George, Benj. G.	Susan F. Shearman	
2 Mch. 1837	George, Wm. P.	Lucy A. West	
25 Jan. 1837	George,, War. S.C.	Louisa A.C. Kidd	Son of Jesse George
26 Sept. 1837	George, John	Mary S. Currell	
5 Feb. 1842	George, Mich. W.	Ann S. Gaine	
5 Dec. 1842	George, Leroy N.	Harriett L. Boatman	Dau. Judith Boatman
9 May 1843	George, Wm. P.	Mary A. Palmer	
23 Nov. 1844	George, Octav. son of Maria George	Frances A. Towles	Dau. of Oliver & Keturah Towles
1 Jan. 1846	George, James	Ann Hammond	
14 June 1844	George, Wm. H.	Mary Ann Flippo	
13 Dec. 1849	George, Jas. L.	Lucy E. Brent	
11 Dec. 1701	Gibson, Rd.	Mrs. Ruth Wright	Widow of Mottrom Wright
27 July 1803	Gibson, John	Polly R. Hunton	

Page 28

DATE	GROOM	BRIDE	PARENTS
9 July 1822	Gibson, Wm.	Margaret L. Lawson	
28 June 1801	Gill, George	Peggy Ball	
3 Sept. 1722	Gilbert, Ezek. of York Co.	Winifred Gibson	Dau. Robt. Gibson
1 Aug. 1749	Gilbert, Ezek.	Eliz. Lawson	
26 June 1722	Gilbreath, Robt.	Margaret Carter (widow)	
30 June 1796	Gilmour, Jno. M.	Cordelia Ball	
15 Feb. 1810	Gilmour, Robt.	Sally McTyre	
2 Oct. 1823	Gilmour, Wm.	Frances Downman	
13 Apr. 1726	Glascock, Geo. of Richmond Co.	Mrs. Judith Ball	Dau. of Wm. Ball
10 Apr. 1728	Glascock, Wm. of Richmond Co.	Mrs. Easter Ball	Dau. of Sarah Ball
13 Jan. 1748	Glascock, George of Richmond Co.	Judith Mitchell	
20 Jan. 1762	Glascock, Wm.	Eliz. Chichester	
20 Jan. 1759	Glascock, Thos.	Mary Ball	
18 Nov. 1779	Glascock, Geo.	--------------	John Hunton, sec.
5 Sept. 1800	Glascock, Rd.	Mrs. Ann S. Brent	
24 Feb. 1802	Glascock, Geo.	Frances B. Berryman	Dau. Sarah Berryman
4 Apr. 1808	Glascock, Rd. M. of Richmond Co.	Frances Fox Edmonds not 21 yrs of age	Dau. Elias Edmonds
11 May 1850	Glascock, J. D.	Lucy Jane George	
28 Aug. 1818	Good, James	Frances Shelton (Chilton ?)	
28 Mch. 1823	Good, Edmund	Mary Chilton	
19 Nov. 1764	Goodridge, Rd.	Ann Reveer	
17 Dec. 1793	Goodridge, Wm. of Orange Co.	Catherine Martin Hinton	
19 Nov. 1795	Goodridge, Wm. (Bachelor)	Ann Flint	
13 Aug. 1777	Gordon, Jas., Jr.	Eliz. Gordon	Sister of Jas Gordon
31 Oct. 1787	Gordon, John	Betty Lee Ball	Jos. Ball, gr. fath.
17 Dec. 1832	Gordon, Jas. T.	Nancy Mitchell	Dau. Thad Mitchell

Page 29

DATE	GROOM	BRIDE	PARENTS
2 Oct. 1844	Gordon, Jos.	Mary Ann Brown	
3 Apr. 1774	Graham, Reginald	Mary Ball (widow)	
24 Apr. 1798	Gresham, Geo.	Mary James	
19 Oct. 1807	Gresham, John	Margaret Chowning	
16 May 1831	Gresham, Samuel	Mrs. Sarah C. Chilton Widow of Fauntler Chilton and sister of Rd. Mitchell	
17 Oct. 1842	Gresham, Jas. W.	Ann E. R. Armstrong	
21 Sept. 1847	Gresham, Jno. F.	Margaret M. Hughlett	
5 Oct. 1734	Griffin, Capt. LeRoy of Richmond Co.	Mrs. Mary Ann Bertrand	Dau. Wm. Bertrand
18 July 1764	Griffin, Leroy of Rd. Co.	Alice Currie	Dau. David Currie
3 Nov. 1772	Griffin, LeRoy	Judith Ball	Dau. Jos. Ball
6 May 1768	Griggs, Thos.	Judith Kirk	Dau. Sarah Kirk
1 Oct. 1772	Griggs, Thos.	Alcey Carter	Dau. Thos. Carter
1 Nov. 1777	Griggs, Wm.	Ruth Everitt (widow)	
20 Apr. 1796	Gundry, John, Sr.	Eliz. Ellett	
18 Feb. 1817	Gundry, John	Judith H. Talley	
13 May 1844	Gundry, John M.	Mrs. Harriet J. George	Dau. Sarah Ball
16 May 1717	Hack, Nich., of Northumberland Co.	Eliz. Howson	
23 Apr. 1746	Hack, Tunstall of Maryland	Miss Hannah Conway of Christ Church Parish	
2 Dec. 1834	Hackney, Rd.	Felicia Kesterson	
18 Dec. 1824	Hale, Francis T. of Fauquier Co.	Olicia T. Ball	Dau. Mary Ball
1 Jan. 1817	Hall, Addison	Susan Edmonds	
13 Sept. 1825	Hall, John	Mary T. A. Gibson	
26 Mch. 1839	Hamilton, John	Louisa D. Hill	
17 June 1784	Hammond, Jas.	Catherine Tapscott	
30 Nov. 1789	Hammond, John	Jean Chowning	
29 Feb. 1792	Hammond, John (widower)	Mary Hazard (widow)	

DATE	GROOM	BRIDE	PARENTS
6 Nov. 1792	Hammond, Thos.	Mary Lewis Tapscott	
9 Aug. 1793	Hammond, Chas.	Ann Gibson Carter	dau. of Eliz. Carter
21 Nov. 1796	Hammond, Jas. (widower)	Winifred Boyd	
14 June 1802	Hammond, Jesse	Nancy Chilton	
7 June 1814	Hammond, Jas.	Eliz. Dameron	
6 July 1818	Hammond, Wm.	Catherine Dunton	Dau. Sarah Dunton
10 Oct. 1820	Hammond, Lewis	Lucy Hammond	
5 Aug. 1840	Hammond, Jas.	Sarah Edwards	
11 Mch. 1845	Hammond, G. B.	Lucy R. Haydon (over 21)	
19 Nov. 1816	Hanks, John	Eliz. Newgent	
12 July 1774	Harcum, Wm. W.	Patty Williams	
21 Jan. 1821	Harcum, Samuel	Polly Gresham	
15 Sept. 1826	Harcum, Wm. P.	Frances H. Towill	Dau. Mark Towill
13 Sept. 1791	Harding, Cyrus of Northumberland	Mary Goodridge	Dau. Rd. & Mary Goodridge
27 Dec. 1827	Harding, John H.	Frances Jose. Lemoine	Dau. F. Lemoine, Sr.
26 Aug. 1826	Harding, Jas.	Frances McNamara	
6 Sept. 1841	Harding Wm. H.	Ann George	
23 May 1806	Harmon, Dan. H.	Sarah George	
18 May 1717	Harrison, Rd.	Ann Reade	
18 Aug. 1769	Harvey, Mungo	Priscilla Ball	
15 May 1815	Harvey, Onesiph.	Rebecca M. George	
6 Mch. 1822	Harvey, Onesiph.	Felicia Towles	
18 Nov. 1772	Hathaway, Thos.	Eliz. Kirk	
15 Aug. 1798	Hathaway, Wm.	Molley Currell	
28 Dec. 1801	Hathaway, John	Jenny P. Newby	Dau. Eliz. Newby
Aug. 1804	Hathaway, Thos.	Jiney Chowning	
11 Mch. 1820	Hathaway, Lawson	Agnes Locke	
16 Nov. 1846	Hathaway, Henry	Harriet E. Edmonds	

DATE	GROOM	BRIDE	PARENTS
18 June 1795	Hawkins, John (planter)	Sarah Cornelius (age 22)	
30 May 1788	Haydon, Ezekiel	Lucy Doggett	Consent Wm. Doggett
29 Dec. 1788	Haydon, John	Elizabeth Potts	Consent Sarah Potts
14 Mch. 1792	Haydon, Wm.	Peggy Sullivant (b. May 10, 1771)	Dau. Judith Sullivant
2 Jan. 1793	Haydon, Chas.	Nancy Myers (widow)	
20 Jan. 1794	Haydon, Wm.	Mary Ann Doggett	
28 Jan. 1801	Haydon, Willis	Eliz. Carter	Dau. Spencer Carter
6 Apr. 1805	Haydon, Thos.	Polly Sampson	Dau. Nancy Sampson
3 Apr. 1810	Haydon, Armistead	Nancy P. Haydon	
15 Apr. 1811	Haydon, Lewis	Alice Hurst	Dau. Jane Hurst
27 June 1828	Haydon, Ezekiel	Eliz. W. Cox	Dau. John Cox
4 Feb. 1833	Haydon, Warner	Dolly Barnett	
9 May 1835	Haydon, Jos.	Lucy B. Hammond	Dau. Eliz. Hammond
15 Aug. 1815	Haydon, Hiram	Mary Treakle	
12 Jan. 1843	Haydon, Hiram	Alice Ashbourne	Dau. Griffin Ashbourne
16 Oct. 1747	Hainie, Wm. of Northumberland Co.	Ann Edwards, (widow)	Sister of Thos. Edwards, Jr.
16 June 1766	Haney, Bridgar	Sarah Shearman	
7 Nov. 1774	Haynie, John	Ann Conway Tapscott	
9 Sept. 1779	Haynie, Daniel of Northumberland	Judith Fleet	
16 Mch. 1781	Haynie, Samuel	Ann Pines Carter	
17 Dec. 1816	Haynie, Cyrus	Judith Lunsford	
2 Jan. 1837	Haynie, Warner	Lucy P. Carpenter	Dau. Lucy Carpenter
20 Dec. 1847	Haynie, Yarrett	Amanda M. Norris	
1 Jan. 1850	Haynie, Jos.	Elizabeth Norris	
26 Feb. 1850	Haynie, Hiram	Lydia Haynie	

Page 32

DATE	GROOM	BRIDE	PARENT
24 June 1812	Hayes, Thos. J.	Eliz. Mitchell	
10 Dec. 1792	Hazard, Elias	Mary Rogers	
19 Dec. 1796	Hazard, Alex.	Judith Davenport	
22 Dec. 1824	Hazard, Cyrus	Polly Hill	
21 Jan. 1836	Hazard, Wm.	Frances Bryant	
23 Mch. 1841	Hazard, Jos.	Mary Eliz. Ashburn	
7 Sept. 1841	Hazard, Henry	Harriett Alfriend	
19 Apr. 1845	Hazzard, Cyrus	Mary N. Spilman	
4 Aug. 1842	Headley, Wm. W.	Juliet A. Riveer	Dau. Mary Riveer
22 July 1734	Heale, Wm.	Sarah Swan	
14 Jan. 1746	Heale, Geo.	Mrs. Sarah Smith	Consent of Jos. & Priscilla Chinn
12 Apr. 1797	Hendley, John	Hannah Doggett	
6 Oct. 1829	Hening, John S.	Mary E. L. Brent	Eliz. L. McNamara guard.
9 July 1733	Hill, John of Northumberland	Eliz. Martin	
25 Dec. 1781	Hill, James	Betty Stephens	
21 Dec. 1786	Hill, James	Nancy Connally	
24 Dec. 1803	Hill, Wm.	Mary Merryman	Dau. of Ann Potts
19 Sept. 1814	Hill, John	Alice Pitman	
12 Jan. 1815	Hill, Wm.	Winny Chilton Moore	
13 Feb. 1817	Hill, Eppa	Polly Chowning Carter	
22 Dec. 1824	Hill, Thos. P.	Milly E. Carter	Dau. James Carter
31 Aug. 1825	Hill, John	Harriett Yopp	
21 Dec. 1829	Hill, Thos.	Ailcey Spilman	
18 Sept. 1839	Hill, Jas. M.	Catherine E. S. Dix	
22 Jan. 1800	Hipkins, Robt. S.	Ann Ball	
15 June 1815	Hilton, Wm.	Ann Warwick	
23 June 1766	Hinton, Henry	Anna Fleet	Dau. of John Fleet

Page 33

DATE	GROOM	BRIDE	PARENTS
17 Nov. 1768	Hinton, Fleet	Catherine Pope	
30 Dec. 1774	Hinton, Thos.	Eliz. Hinton, widow	
19 July 1798	Hinton, Rd.	Mary Ingram	
21 Dec. 1798	Hinton, John	Molly Brooks	Edmond Brooks consent
15 Nov. 1813	Hinton, Archib.	Nancy Kent	
24 Mch. 1824	Hinton, Wm.	Judith Hill	
13 Nov. 1834	Hinton, Geo.	Catherine Kent	
13 Dec. 1842	Hinton, Jas. W.	Eliz. Francis	
16 Oct. 1850	Hinton, Archib.	Sarah Masden	
28 June 1723	Hobson, Wm. of Northumberland	Judith Fleet	
6 Dec. 1828	Holliday, Needham	Amanda M. Robertson	
12 Dec. 1845	Holmes, John	Polly E. Buchan	Dau. Nicholas Buchan
4 Aug. 1719	Horton, Robt.	Blanche Kelly	
18 May 1717	Howson, Rd.	Anne Reade	
10 Nov. 1722	Howson, Leonard of Northumberland	Anne Fleet	
15 July 1749	Hubbard, Ephraim	Hannah Edmonds	
17 May 1756	Hubbard, Wm.	Eliz. Boatman	
21 Sept. 1780	Hubbard, Jos.	Rebecca George	
2 Jan. 1783	Hubbard, Thos.	Ann Yopp	
3 Jan. 1785	Hubbard, Wm.	Judith Yopp	
14 Sept. 1786	Hubbard, Elias	Judith George	
13 Jan. 1808	Hubbard, Jabez	Eliz. Kirk	
5 Jan. 1814	Hubbard, Jesse	Polly B. James	Dau. of B. James
21 Nov. 1836	Hudnall, Alfred	Jane O. Beane	
12 Dec. 1779	Hudson, Geo.	Eliz. West	
17 Mch. 1786	Hudson, Henry	Amia Pitman	
16 Sept. 1799	Hughs, Thos.	Judith Hill	

Page 34

DATE	GROOM	BRIDE	PARENTS
3 Sept. 1788	Hughlett, Yarret	Sally Berryman	Dau. Sarah Berryman
21 May 1801	Hughlett, Ephraim	Barbara Spillman	
28 July 1806	Hughlett, August.	Sarah George	
28 Dec. 1806	Hughlett, Ephraim	Molly George	
19 Dec. 1808	Hughlett, John	Roxillana Spiller	
19 Dec. 1809	Hughlett, Martin	Alice Pusley	Dau. Chas. & Hannah Pusley
7 Jan. 1813	Hughlett, Bede	Hannah Oliver	
2 Dec. 1813	Hughlett, Martin	Lucy Webb	
31 Dec. 1811	Hughlett, Royston 21 Jan. 1st	Nancy Short	
19 Mch. 1818	Hughlett, Royston	Lucy Pollard Hill	Dau. of Mary Hill
10 July 1824	Hughlett, Royston	Lucy Haydon	
29 June 1829	Hughlett, Wm. E.	Margaret M. Mitchell	
8 May 1833	Hughlett, Bede	Polly Haydon	
4 Jan. 1848	Hughlett, Robt.	Caroline S. Kirk	Dau. Eliz. Kirk
19 Feb. 1822	Hull, John	Sally Ball	
28 Apr. 1797	Hundley, John	Hannah Doggett	
31 Dec. 1844	Huner, Waring	Mary Ingram	Dau. of Thos. Ingram
22 Dec. 1774	Hunt, John	Eliz. Lawson	
16 Mch. 1779	Hunt, John	Ellen Blade	
24 June 1796	Hunt, John (bachelor)	Lucinda Brent	
13 Nov. 1722	Hunton, Thos.	Mary Currill (widow)	
15 Nov. 1734	Hunton, Thos.	Anne Wale	
30 Dec. 1774	Hunton, Thomas	Eliz. Hinton (widow)	
20 May 1779	Hunton, Thos.	Betty Yerby	
18 Nov. 1779	Hunton, John	Hannah Carter	
16 Mch. 1789	Hunton, Thos.	Ann Pope	

Page 35

DATE	GROOM	BRIDE	PARENTS
15 May 1794	Hunton, Jno. Wise	Mary Pollard	Dau. of Jas. Pollard
28 July 1819	Hunton, John W.	Mary Hutchinson	
30 Apr. 1821	Hunton, Jno. W.	Ann Doggett	
24 Oct. 1827	Hunton, Jno. W.	Nancy Dunnaway	
15 Oct. 1801	Hurst, Warner	Susan Spiller	
17 Mch. 1806	Hurst, Isaac	Nancy Lawson	
21 Jan. 1823	Hurst, John	Cordelia Norris	
21 Nov. 1843	Hurst, Jas.	Athaliah A. Jones	
21 Jan. 1778	Hutchings, John	Sally Miller	
19 Dec. 1791	Hutchings, Rd.	Milly Beane	Dau. of John Beane
17 Mch. 1794	Hutchins, John	Eliz. Tankersley	Dau. of Geo. Tankersley
16 Aug. 1813	Hutchings, Rd.	Molly Blakemore	
16 Nov. 1818	Hutchings, John	Polly Biscoe	
16 Dec. 1822	Hutchings, Rd.	Eliz. K. Hathaway	
23 Dec. 1822	Hutchings, Hugh	Nancy Biscoe	
14 Oct. 1836	Hutchings, Thos.	Louisa A. Yerby	
8 Jan. 1805	Hutchinson, Hill W.	Molly Pearson	
16 Apr. 1772	Ingram, Thos.	Sarah Fleet	
15 Apr. 1799	Ingram, Chas.	Eliz. Garton	Dau. of Rachel Crowder
13 Dec. 1802	Ingram, Jno. F.	Susanna Hinton	Dau. of Ann Hinton
12 Aug. 1811	Ingram, John	Ann M. Brent	
16 June 1825	Ingram, Jas.	Leah Hinton	
19 Dec. 1825	Ingram, Geo.	Martha Ann Johnson	Dau. Ralph Johnson
6 Nov. 1826	Ingram, Wm. S.	Tomasey S. Callahan	
29 June 1827	Ingram, Thos.	Sarah Hinton	
24 Nov. 1829	Ingram, Wm. S.	Eliz. Lattimore	
13 May 1834	Ingram, Wm.	Mary E. Kellam	
1 Jan. 1836	Ingram, Thos. S.	Rebecca M. James	

DATE	GROOM	BRIDE	PARENTS
22 Jan. 1835	Ingram, Griffin	Mary A. D. Flowers	
30 Dec. 1836	Ingram, Jas.	Sally L. Flippen	
11 May 1837	Ingram, Sam. M.	Anna B. Robertson	
31 Jan. 1837	Ingram, Griffin	Frances H. Selba	
1 Jan. 1840	Ingram, Chas.	Margaret Ann Beane	
22 July 1841	Ingram, Chas.	Mary C. Biscoe	
16 Apr. 1794	Isles, Absolem	Betsy Webb	
17 June 1805	Jackson, Benj.	Sally Jones	
20 Dec. 1763	James, Bartley	Mrs. Eliz. Waugh	
13 Apr. 1780	James, Wm.	Mary Ellett	
20 Jan. 1790	James, Matthias	Judith Hinton	
16 Feb. 1795	James, Bartley	Amy Yopp	
7 Sept. 1795	James, Thos.	Eliz. Brent (widow)	
7 Jan. 1804	James Chas.	Sally Hubbard	
12 Nov. 1805	James, Robt.	Charlotte Locke	Dau. of Jos. Locke
7 Apr. 1808	James, Wm. H.	Catherine Carter	Dau. Martin Carter
20 Apr. 1811	James, John	Betsy L. Hinton	
25 June 1812	James, Bartley	Susanna Ingram	
10 May 1817	James, Bartley	Sally N. Brent	
17 Apr. 1822	James, Rd.	Eliz. Currill	
5 Aug. 1824	James, Heirom P.	Delia Deams or Davis	Dau. Ruth Deams (Davis)
12 Nov. 1826	James, Capt. Thos.	Judith Marsh	
29 Nov. 1826	James, David H.	Eliz. H. Carter	
15 Apr. 1829	James, Thos., Jr.	Polly B. James	
5 March 1831	James, Thos	Rebecca M. George	
8 Jan. 1834	James, John	Ann Pitman	
29 Nov. 1843	James, Jas. B.	Eliz. C. Lawson	Dau. Judith N. Lawson
1 Jan. 1844	James, Wm. M., Jr.	Margaret Ann Hinton	

Page 37

DATE	GROOM	BRIDE	PARENTS
8 Oct. 1832	Jefferson, David	Eliz. Mason	
17 Sept. 1798	Jeffries, Wm.	Lucy Sebree	
30 Mch. 1825	Jeffries, Griffin	Eliz. Payne	
2 Dec. 1793	Jesse, Samuel	Catherine George	Dau. Frances George
1 Feb. 1786	Johnson, Geo.	Eliz. Blackmon	
13 Feb. 1795	Johnson, Henry	Ann Weaver	
24 July 1804	Johnson, Wm.	Morning Bond	
14 Mch. 1740	Jones, Wm. of Northumberland	Ann Bell	Dau. of John Bell
30 Sept. 1747	Jones, John of Middlesex	Sarah Ball	Dau. of Margaret Ball
2 Nov. 1750	Jones, John of Orange Co.	Mary Bell	
18 Dec. 1770	Jones, Francis of Warwick Co.	Jane Armistead	
3 Oct. 1789	Jones, Lewis	Milly Chilton	Dau. of Wm. Chilton
13 June 1794	Jones, Daniel	Rachel Howe	Dau. of Peter Howe
8 Aug. 1795	Jones, David	Rhoda Jones	
17 Dec. 1795	Jones, Jas.	Winifred Boling	
1 Jan. 1802	Jones, Thos.	Judith Sorrell	
17 Apr. 1822	Jones, John	Betsy Weaver	
30 June 1830	Jones, Wm.	Frances Gilmour	
19 Dec. 1831	Jones, John	Betsy Bell	
8 Nov. 1837	Jones, Wmson C.	Athaliah Ann Mitchell	
30 Oct. 1839	Jones, Henry	Margaret Lewin	
7 Apr. 1846	Jones, Wm. E.	Mary Francis	
15 Feb. 1849	Jones, Martin	Jane Nickens	
7 Feb. 1849	Jones, Opie	Eliza Nickens	
9 Mch. 1849	Jones, Elias	Harriett Jordan	
23 Jan. 1833	Jordan, John	Harriett Lewin	
2 Nov. 1721	Keene, Wm. of Northumberland	Eliz. Ball	

Page 38

DATE	GROOM	BRIDE	PARENTS
14 Apr. 1749	Keene, Newton	Sarah Edwards	
6 Apr. 1745	Kelley, Wm.	Eliz. Riley (widow)	
16 July 1778	Kelley, Jas.	Judith Cammell	
5 Jan. 1792	Kelly, John	Sarah Norris	
21 Jan. 1799	Kelly, Jas.	Hannah H. George	
26 Jan. 1799	Kelley, Jas.	Hannah H. Tapscott	
21 Nov. 1842	Kelley, Jas. W.	Amy Y. Hubbard	
12 May 1847	Kelly, John	Sally Veney	
5 Dec. 1780	Kem, Jos.	Amy David	
23 Dec. 1783	Kem, Henry	Joannah Robinson	
1 Dec. 1788	Kem, Henry	Eliza Schofield	
16 Dec. 1801	Kemm, Rd.	Sally B. Brown	
1 Feb. 1803	Kemm, Burges	Lucy Edwards	
24 Dec. 1817	Kemm, Jas.	Milly Brown	
20 Oct. 1823	Kemm, John	Mary Hazard	
24 Dec. 1828	Kemm, Rd. R.	Winifred Thomas	
13 Oct. 1830	Kem, John	Alice H. Oliver	
9 Oct. 1833	Kemm, John	Eliz. Davis	
7 Apr. 1847	Kem, Jno. E.	Maria H. Ball	
9 Sept. 1801	Kemp, John	Chrissy Cox	
24 Sept. 1829	Kemp, John	Finnette Chilton	
11 Oct. 1774	Kenner, Wm.	Betty Myars	
3 Dec. 1844	Kenner, Waring	Mary Ingram	Dau. of Thos. Ingram
21 Dec. 1780	Kent, Wm.	Ann Taylor	
1 Sept. 1787	Kent, Wm.	Sarah Chilton	
16 Apr. 1795	Kent, Thos.(mariner)	Priscilla Doggett	
13 July 1795	Kent, Wm.	Eliz. James	Dau. of Eliz. James
22 Dec. 1800	Kent, John	Mary Mahanes	

Page 39

DATE	GROOM	BRIDE	PARENTS
22 Dec. 1803	Kent, W. B.	Jenny Lee McTyre	
15 Mch. 1809	Kent, Rhodam	Sally O. Stott	Dau. of Eliz. Stott
11 Apr. 1809	Kent, John of Northumberland	Nancy Towell	Dau. of Mark Towell
18 Dec. 1809	Kent, Jesse	Fanny Brook	
8 July 1809	Kent, Capt. Dan.	Mary Hunton	
19 Mch. 1810	Kent, Lody W.	Caty Brooks	
19 Dec. 1826	Kent, Wm. B.	Nancy Buchan	
1 Nov. 1832	Kent, Jesse	Harriett Hill	
22 May 1838	Kent, Dan.	Frances Ann Edmonds	
17 Dec. 1838	Kent, Beverley	Ann C. Danson	
30 Mch. 1787	Kesterson, Wm.	Sally Kent	
4 Feb. 1801	Kesterson, Jas.	Kitty Chinn Carter	Dau. of Jos. Carter
16 Apr. 1804	Kesterson, Jas.	Kitty Chowning	
13 Sept. 1821	Kesterson, W. A.	Eliza S. P. Mitchell	Dau. of Geo. Mitchel
13 Dec. 1831	Key, Geo.	Jane Veney	
30 Dec. 1835	Kee, Wm. H.	Polly Pinn	
26 Dec. 1848	Keser, Monroe	Catherine Cox	
1 Aug. 1798	Kidd, Benj. (widower)	Frances C. Tapscott (widow)	
9 Jan. 1832	Kidd, Robt. B.	Caroline Chowning	Consent of J. Chowning
4 May 1747	Kirk, Anthony	Sarah Brent	
27 Aug. 1762	Kirk, Jas.	Mary Norris	
19 May 1768	Kirk, Jas.	Lucey Carter	
20 May 1784	Kirk, Geo.	Sally Brent	
19 Jan. 1789	Kirk, Anthony	Eliz. Fenley	
25 Feb. 1801	Kirk, John	Sally Pollard	
22 Feb. 1816	Kirk, Westley	Eliz. Pullen	

Page 40

DATE	GROOM	BRIDE	PARENTS
9 Aug. 1830	Kirk, Wm. H.	Eliz. M. Myers	
22 Dec. 1801	Kirkham, Wm.	Eliz. G. Wilson	
2 Jan. 1803	Kirkham, John	Hannah Brent	
18 Dec. 1805	Kirkham, John	Eliz. Hill	
8 May 1839	Kirkham, Braxton	Sarah Hathaway (over 21 yrs.)	
4 Nov. 1803	Kirkmyer, Fred.	Eliz. Scurlock	
27 Apr. 1831	Kirkmyer, Fred.	Catherine Carter	
23 Dec. 1833	Kirkmyer, Geo.	Catherine M. Saunders	
24 Nov. 1785	Knight, John	Eliz. Riveer	
4 Dec. 1822	Knight, John	Lucy G. Talley	
12 Oct. 1780	Lamkin, Chattin	Betty Miller	
28 Jan. 1803	Langsdale, John	Betsy W. Spriggs	
3 Mch. 1831	Laws, Wm.	Louisa Lewis	
14 Mch. 1849	Laws, Leroy	Betsy Lewin	
21 Oct. 1768	Lawson, Henry	Esther Chinn	Robt. Chinn consent
27 Dec. 1793	Lawson, John	Charlotte Ashburn	Dau. of Margaret Ashburn
20 Jan. 1794	Lawson, John	Mary Tunstall Degge	
28 Jan. 1796	Lawson, Henry C.	Margaret S. Lee	
19 July 1802	Lawson, Anthony	Ann Shelton	
19 Dec. 1810	Lawson, Eppa	Ann Thornton Longwith	
28 Nov. 1821	Lawson, Thos. L.	Judith N. Brent	Dau. of Alice Brent
23 Jan. 1826	Lawson, Henry B.	Sally E. McNamara	
1 Sept. 1847	Lawson, Jas.	Eliz. Barrick	
9 Jan. 1770	Leadford, Jas. of Northumberland	---- Garlington	Dau. of Eliz. Garlington
30 Nov. 1807	Ledford, John	Judith M. George	
8 Nov. 1721	Lee, Chas. of Northumberland	Eliz. Pinckard	
20 Dec. 1749	Lee, John of Essex.	Mary Ball	

Page 41

DATE	GROOM	BRIDE	PARENTS
9 July 1749	Lee, Kendall of Northumberland	Betty Heale	Dau. of Priscilla Chinn
10 Jan. 1778	Lee, Richard E.	Letty Kelley	Sister of Geo. Kelly
1 Feb. 1780	Lee, Thos.	Eliz. Currell	
9 Dec. 1782	Lee, Chas.	Mildred Henning	
18 Sept. 1783	Lee, Rd.	Lucy Denny	
10 Feb. 1787	Lee, Geo. of Northumberland	Frances Ball	
3 June 1802	Lee, Thos.	Sally Hill	
27 Nov. 1828	Lee, Wm. H.	Harriet S. Ball	
17 Dec. 1832	Lee, John L.	Eliz. I. Ball	
6 Feb. 1841	Lee, Geo. G.	Ann Mary Carpenter	
20 Jan. 1762	Leeland, John of Northumberland	Lucy Lee	
19 Oct. 1775	Leland, John, Jr.	Judith Smith	
13 Dec. 1797	Leland, Chas. (widower)	Sarah Towles	
27 Feb. 1806	Leland, Baldwin M.	Eliz. Haggeman	Dau. of Mary Ann Haggeman
28 Feb. 1807	Leland, Leroy P.	Ann G. Haggeman	Dau. of Mary Ann Haggeman
30 Nov. 1841	Leland, Leroy G.	Ann N. Hubbard	
14 Sept. 1842	Leland, Dr. Chas. H.	Susan C. Waddy	
Aug. 1803	Lemoine, Feriel	Fanny Mitchell	
1 Jan. 1805	Lewin, Chas.	Polly Armistead Nickens	
24 Mch. 1819	Lewin, John	Betsy Pinn	
3 Feb. 1836	Lewin, Leroy	Nancy Pinn	Dau. of Nancy Pinn
19 July 1848	Lewin, Leroy	Arreller Weaver	
7 Jan. 1768	Lewis, Wm.	Anne Sharpe	Dau. of Sarah Bond
7 Jan. 1768	Lewis, John of Northumberland	Ann S. Lawson	
4 Dec. 1850	Lewis, Jas. W.	Jane Lewin	

Page 42

DATE	GROOM	BRIDE	PARENTS
6 Dec. 1771	Lightburne, Henry	Eliz. Currell	Dau. of Geo. & Eliz. Currell
26 Dec. 1806	Lyburn, Wm.	Darky Bell	
17 Feb. 1849	Liburn, Wm.	Mary Blueford	
17 Feb. 1849	Liburn, Samuel	Mary Wood	
18 Feb. 1734	Linsey, Opie	Sarah Heale	Dau. of Geo. Heale
2 Jan. 1795	Little, Wm.	Nancy Blackmore	
6 July 1785	Lock, Jos.	Molly Beane	
6 Mch 1827	Locke, Ludwell I.	Sally S. Currell	
14 Jan. 1830	Locke, Addison	Eliz. Beane	
24 May 1839	Locke, Addison	Mary Ann Lee	Dau. of Arthur Lee
17 June 1793	Longwith, John	Eliz. Wilder	
6 Oct. 1818	Longwith, John	Molly Williams	
13 Feb. 1823	Longworth, Burges	Sally Tankersley	
21 Nov. 1826	Longworth, John	Eliz. James	
20 June 1828	Longworth, Wm.	Harriett Trott	
23 Feb. 1834	Longworth, Burges	Leanna Walker	
11 June 1840	Longworth, John	Mary P. James	
13 Nov. 1745	Lowrey, Gawin	Bethelen Newsom (widow)	
9 May 1777	Lowrey, Gawin	Hannah Chowning (widow)	
24 Dec. 1791	Lowrey, John	Betty Hill	
24 Mch. 1815	Lowrey, John	Judith Darby	
10 Dec. 1827	Lowrey, John	Jane Stott	
4 July 1780	Luckham, John	Mary Bennet	
11 Aug. 1789	Luckham, Wm.	Judith Arms	
17 Feb. 1849	Luckum, Thos.	Milly Veney	
19 Feb. 1762	Lunsford, Moses of Northumberland	Anne Payne	
26 Feb. 1774	Lunsford, Rhodam	Lettice Carter (widow)	
11 Nov. 1772	Lunsford, Edwin	Mary Carter	

Page 43

DATE	GROOM	BRIDE	PARENTS
21 Mch. 1783	Lunsford, John	Sarah Ellen Carter	
8 July 1794	Lunsford, Rhodam, Jr.	Sally Cox	Dau. of Thos. Cox
5 Aug. 1795	Lunsford, Epa.	Chloe Yopp	
18 Aug. 1803	Lunsford, Linton	Franky Carter	Dau. Jas. Carter
6 May 1808	Lunsford, Epa.	Seilah L. Fendley	Dau. of Sarah Fendley
8 Jan. 1811	Lunsford, Moses	Sally Lunsford	Dau. of John Lunsford
17 Nov. 1817	Lunsford, Jno. Jr.	Lettice L. Carter	
11 June 1819	Lunsford, Moses of Northumberland	Margaret Edwards	
11 Oct. 1821	Lunsford, Eppa	Mary Briant Warwick	
6 Dec. 1831	Lunsford, Warner C.	Ann M. Doggett	
6 Apr. 1836	Lunsford, Chas.	Eliz. Weaver	
11 June 1724	Lyell, John	Mary Taylor	Dau. of Ann Burn
11 July 1744	McAdams, Jos. of Northumberland	Sarah Ann Pickard (widow)	
22 Sept. 1724	McCarty, Dennis of Northumberland	Sarah Ball	Dau. of Wm. Ball
19 May 1758	McCarty, Thad.	Ann Ghinn	
23 Oct. 1818	McCarty, Wm. D.	Frances R. Carter	
28 Oct. 1839	McClanahan, Thos. H.	Ann Hinton	
30 Jan. 1850	McCoy, Fleet M.	Mary Ann Flood	
10 Apr. 1772	McCroskey, Sam. S.	Charlotte Taylor	Adopted dau. of Thos. Pinckard
18 Feb. 1843	McKenney, Jos. M.	Dorcas J. Talley	
6 Aug. 1796	McNamara, Tim (mariner)	Mary Lawson	
30 Aug. 1804	McNamara, John	Winifred R. Lawson	
15 July 1807	McNamara, Tim.	Frances Lawson	
16 Jan. 1817	McNamara, John	Sally M. Gibson	
20 Nov. 1820	McNamara, Capt. Tim.	Eliz. L. Brent	
20 Dec. 1830	McNamara, Henry	Rosetta Johnson	Consent of Jno. & Eliz. Johnson

Page 44

DATE	GROOM	BRIDE	PARENTS
22 May 1772	MacTire, John	Sally Henning	
21 June 1782	McTyre, John	Molly Doggett	
15 Oct. 1795	McTyre, Chas. L.	Eliz. Davenport	
17 Dec. 1825	McTyre, John	Nancy Hill	
19 Aug. 1732	McNeal, Arthur	Eliz. Frizell (widow)	
20 Nov. 1846	Madison, Eldred	Decyenthia F. Payne	
12 Sept. 1785	Marsh, Gideon	Milly Angell (age 23)	
26 Jan. 1796	Marsh, Wm.	Hetty Kem	
8 Mch. 1795	March, Wm.	Mildred Moore	
27 Mch. 1808	Marsh, Roy. C.	Mary Boyd	
3 June 1836	Marsh, Jas.	Mary Carter	
30 Oct. 1821	Marshall, Chas.	Judith Steptoe	
16 Aug. 1782	Martin, Wm.	Hannah Mitchell	
8 Mch. 1785	Mash, Wm.	Mildred Moore	
18 Jan. 1796	Mash, Wm.	Betty Kem (widow)	
19 Jan. 1788	Mason, Peter	Nancy Davis	
26 Aug. 1789	Mason, Peter	Thomasin Davis	
1 Oct. 1790	Mason, Thos.	Margaret James	
19 May 1794	Mason, Thos.	Leannah Cornelius (widow of Wm. Cornelius)	
30 Apr. 1794	Mason, Thos. (widower)	Nancy Stott (widow)	
24 Dec. 1800	Mason, Peter	Sally Sebree	
12 Apr. 1802	Mason, John	Sally Jones	Son of Alley Mason
12 Sept. 1805	Mason, Peter	Polly Sagathy	
29 Jan. 1818	Mason, John	Elis. Beachum Weymouth	
6 Jan. 1819	Mason, Thos.	Lucy H. Thrall	
19 Dec. 1831	Mason, Wm.	Rebecca H. James	
16 Mch. 1840	Maston, John	Sarah Robbins	

Page 45

DATE	GROOM	BRIDE	PARENTS
4 Nov. 1835	Mathews, Jas. L.	Louisa A. Ball	
16 Feb. 1775	Maxwell, John	Frances Brent	
5 Sept. 1843	Mealy, Jessee	Frances E. Sebree	
13 Dec. 1782	Meredith, John	Mary Dillard	
18 Nov. 1822	Meredith, John, Maj.	Ann C. Towill	
11 Dec. 1828	Meredith, John	Ann Steptoe Brent	
11 Aug. 1803	Merryman, Thos.	Milley Davis	Dau. of Jos. Davis
11 Sept. 1805	Merryman, John	Lucinda Blakemore	
8 Sept. 1724	Mileham, Sam.	Martha Gardner	
10 Dec. 1718	Miller, Wm.	Martha Taylor	
23 Dec. 1800	Miller, Peter	Sally Everett Newby	Son of Jno. Miller, Sr.
10 Aug. 1808	Miller, Thos.	Sally Swanson	
22 Feb. 1841	Miller, Jas. R.	Sarah B. James	
25 Jan. 1850	Mills, Levin	Nancy Cornelius	
9 Dec. 1754	Milner, Francis	Betty Ball	
3 Aug. 1744	Mitchell, John	Charity Coleman	
7 Sept. 1746	Mitchell, Robt. the younger	Hannah Ball	
24 Nov. 1769	Mitchell, Wm.	Mary Miller	
7 Mch. 1783	Mitchell, Rd.	Peggy Gunyon	
1 May 1800	Mitchell, Dan. P.	Catherine C. Degge	
22 July 1800	Mitchell, Rd.	Dolly Degges	
23 Sept. 1801	Mitchell, Jas.	Susanna F. Shearman	Dau. of Susanna Shearman
8 Nov. 1804	Mitchell, Thad.	Ann Mitchell	
24 Feb. 1808	Mitchell, Dan. P.	Eliz. George	
15 Dec. 1808	Mitchell, Henry M.	Eliz. Brent	
18 Dec. 1809	Mitchell, Jas.	Eleanor B. Brent	
24 Dec. 1812	Mitchell, Thad.	Eliz. Campbell	

Page 46

DATE	GROOM	BRIDE	PARENTS
30 May 1815	Mitchell, Wm. B.	Margaret Dowman	
17 Sept. 1823	Mitchell, Rd.	Frances Stubblefield	
10 Nov. 1825	Mitchell, Jos. B.	Henrietta S. Kesterson	Dau. of Kitty Kesterson
13 Dec. 1827	Mitchell, Dan. P.	Virginia P. Miller	
23 June 1834	Mitchell, Geo. W.	Polly Carter	
18 Nov. 1834	Mitchell, Rd.	Frances Edwards	
17 Nov. 1837	Mitchell, Dan. P.	Jane E. George	
4 Oct. 1845	Mitchell, Rd. B.	Tomaza S. Gresham	
16 Oct. 1727	Montague, Wm.,-Jr.	Mrs. Hannah Ball	Son of Wm. Montague Dau. Sarah Ball
27 Jan. 1749	Montague, Wm.	Jane B. Ballendine	
20 June 1760	Montague, Jas.	Eliza Chinn	
11 Dec. 1772	Montague, Wm.	Mrs. Lucy Smith relict Baldwin Smith	
17 Mch. 1801	Montague, Wm.	Frances Downman	
25 Aug. 1781	More, John	Ann Currell	
5 Oct. 1785	Moore, Reuben	Peggy McDaniel	
22 Sept. 1792	Moore, Wm.	Milly Angell (widow)	
21 Dec. 1825	Moore, Chas.	Nancy Percifull	
11 Apr. 1836	Moore, Wm. S.	Lilly T. Blakemore	
4 Aug. 1802	Morrison, Jas.	Anna Crowder	
9 Dec. 1766	Mott, Wm.	Eliz. Hubbard	
21 Feb. 1782	Mott, Thos.	Winifred Doggett	
21 Sept. 1789	Mott. Thos.	Betty Cundiff	
4 Mch. 1796	Mott, Wm.	Lucretia Walker	
15 Oct. 1798	Mott, Jos. Jr.	Molly Sutton	Dau. of Jno. Sutton of Northumberland
20 Dec. 1772	Newby, John	Eliz. Hinton	Dau. of Thos. Hinton
20 Nov. 1813	Newgent, Thos.	Caty Brannan	

Page 47

DATE	GROOM	BRIDE	PARENTS
15 May 1815	Newgent, Thos.	Fanny Lowry	
25 Oct. 1738	Newsome, Robt., Jr.	Behethelen Jones (widow)	
21 Dec. 1834	Newton, Geo.	Ann Mealy	
1 Dec. 1769	Nichols, John	Mary Townsend	
12 Aug. 1786	Nicken, Robt.	Eliz. Gray	
17 Sept. 1791	Nickens, John, Jr.	Ann Mills	
5 Mch. 1793	Nickens, Robt.	Nancy Howe spinster, over 21	
20 Aug. 1806	Nickens, Rd.	Eliz. Hamilton	
21 Jan. 1819	Nickens, Arms.	Polly Weaver	
26 Jan. 1821	Nickens, Jos.	Polly Kent Wiggins	Dau. of Ann Wiggins
23 Dec. 1822	Nickens, Lindsey	Minerva Collins	
12 Jan. 1824	Nickens, Rd.	Mary Lewis	
19 Oct. 1830	Nickens, Lindsay	Rachel C. Veney	
17 Dec. 1835	Nickens, Cyrus	Mary Ann Lewin	
17 May 1837	Nickens, Overton	Judith Veney	
17 Feb. 1849	Nickens, Steptoe	Betsy Veney	
4 Feb. 1737/8	Norris, John	Jane Camell	
3 Aug. 1770	Norris, Geo.	Eliz. Ledford	
3 Oct. 1774	Norris, Wm.	Judith Horton	
19 Dec. 1780	Norris, Martin	Nancy Mercer	
21 Nov. 1789	Norris, Eppa	Molly Arms	Dau. of Jane Arms
11 Jan. 1791	Norris, Rd.	Sarah Ann Newby	
10 Mch. 1792	Norris, Jas.	Judith Mitchell	Dau. of Wm. Mitchell
29 May 1809	Norris, John	Betsy Taylor Norris	Dau. Eppa Norris
17 June 1816	Norris, John	Olivia Carpenter	
19 Dec. 1820	Norris, Rd.	Sarah Stott	
1 May 1832	Norris, Jas., Jr.	Eliz. H. Davenport	

Page 48

DATE	GROOM	BRIDE	PARENTS
3 June 1833	Norris, Thos.	Sarah G. Chowning	Gr.son of Eppa Norris
24 Dec. 1844	Norris, Rd.	Jane Sutton	
26 Dec. 1848	Norris, Wm. O.	Sarah Spilman	
21 Feb. 1839	Northern, Rd.	Kitty Ann Dunnaway	
15 Oct. 1798	Nugent, Thos.	Judith Dunnaway	
16 Nov. 1769	Nutt, Wm. of Northumberland	Mary Downing	
27 Oct. 1781	Nutt, Wm.	Jane Swan Brent	
6 Dec. 1798	Nutt, Wm. D.	Eliz. Chinn	
18 Mch. 1802	Nutt, Leroy	Alcy T. Gallo	
23 Jan. 1815	Nutt, Robt.	Charlotte McA. Taylor	
30 Nov. 1835	Nutt, Jas.	Jane M. Walker	
13 May 1760	Nuttall, Jas.	Sarah James	Dau. of Thos. James
16 Nov. 1775	Nuttall, John	Judith Lawson (spinster)	
2 Feb. 1803	Oldham, Sam.	Ann Shearman	
23 July 1817	Oldham, Wm.	Frances Blakey	
2 Jan. 1839	Oldham, Thos.	Mary L. Blakemore	
28 Feb. 1771	Oliver, Lowry	Ellen Cammell	Dau. of Winifred Cammell
21 Mch. 1780	Oliver, Tapscott	Winifred Lunsford	
17 Aug. 1802	Oliver, Thos.	Hannah Meredith	
24 Dec. 1807	Oliver, Geo. P.	Elizabeth Meredith	
20 Sept. 1813	Oliver, Thos. B.	Sally C. Fendla	Dau. of Sally Fendla
8 Nov. 1818	Oliver, Mat. H.	Polly P. Davis	
28 Nov. 1821	Oliver, Thos. B.	Sally T. Schofield	
13 Jan. 1848	Oliver, Thos. R. M.	Ann C. Beane	Dau. of Aaron Beane
10 Feb. 1734	Opie, Lindsy of Northumberland	Sarah Heale	Dau. of Geo. Heale
11 Dec. 1817	Orrill, Wm.	Polly Simmons Lowry	
21 July 1801	Osborne, John	Rebecca Bourke	Dau. of Mary Bourke

Page 49

DATE	GROOM	BRIDE	PARENTS
18 Feb. 1818	Owens, Thos. M.	Judy Cundiff	Dau. of John Cundiff
26 Dec. 1832	Owens, Wm.	Frances L. Anderson	
20 Oct. 1834	Pace, Geo. D.	Eliz. Hutchings	
3 Mch. 1835	Pace, Wm. K.	Ann Chowning	
26 July 1718	Page, Mann	Judith Carter	
29 July 1785	Palmer, Thos.	Judith Cundiff	
26 Sept. 1785	Palmer, Lott	Nancy Walker	
1 Oct. 1787	Palmer, John	Lucy White	
25 July 1792	Palmer, Lott (widower)	Betty Carter (spinster)	
26 Jan. 1796	Palmer, John	Mary Norris	
7 Sept. 1797	Palmer, R. D.	Molly Cundiff b.Jan. 1776	Dau. Rd. & Susanna Cundiff
17 Apr. 1805	Palmer, Rawleigh	Sally Palmer	
30 May 1805	Palmer, Benj.	Polly George	
13 Mch. 1807	Palmer, Lott	Betsy Swanson	
21 Dec. 1807	Palmer, R. D.	Dolly I. Palmer	
27 Feb. 1817	Palmer, Benj.	Mary George	
9 June 1819	Palmer, Chas.	Eliz. Gresham	
29 July 1847	Palmer, Thos. D.	Ann Knight	
24 Apr. 1811	Parrott, Geo. W.	Eliz. Robertson	
6 Oct. 1718	Pasquett, Jerome	Lycia King	
2 Oct. 1797	Pasquett, John	Eliz. Newby	
13 Oct. 1729	Payne, Geo.	Frances Edmonds	
19 Aug. 1734	Payne, Merrim.	Catherine Brent	Son of Judith Payne
20 June 1757	Payne, John	Jean Christopher	
16 July 1762	Payne, Wm.	Lucy George	
20 Jan. 1764	Payne, Rd.	Ellen Bailey	
30 Mch. 1770	Payne, John	Ellen Payne	

Page 50

DATE	GROOM	BRIDE	PARENTS
17 July 1771	Payne, John	Bridget Blakemore	Dau. of Edward Blakemore
21 Jan. 1773	Payne, Rd.	Alice Shearman	Dau. of Ann Shearman
17 Dec. 1795	Payne, Edward	Sally Davenport	
16 Dec. 1807	Payne, Wm.	Sarah Ann Taylor	Son of R. H. Payne Dau. of Thos. Taylor
11 Aug. 1814	Payne, Edw.	Apphia Palmer	
14 Sept. 1815	Payne, Geo.	Polly Smith Doggett	Dau. John Doggett
30 Nov. 1815	Payne, Wm. J.	Eliz. Chowning	
29 Apr. 1818	Payne, John	Harriett Eustace	
30 Apr. 1835	Payne, Geo. W.	Esther C. Lawson	Dau. Margaret Lawson
3 Mch. 1839	Payne, Thos.	Catherine Currell	
22 Nov. 1843	Payne, Edw.	Eliz. Fendla	
7 Oct. 1788	Pemberton, Larkin	Mary Newby	Dau. Oswald Newby
3 Mch. 1793	Penn, Aaron	Mary Kelly Weaver	Elijah Weaver-father
8 Jan. 1727	Pendleton, Jas. of K. & Q. Co.	Mary Lyell (widow)	
17 Mch. 1787	Percifull, Elij.	Betsy Carter	
16 Jan. 1797	Percifull, Elij. (widower)	Eliz. Reveer Davis (spinster)	
14 Apr. 1812	Percifull, John Y.	Margaret Dunnaway	
30 Dec. 1812	Percifull, Robt.	Nancy Sutton	Peter Beane certifies bride is 21.
26 June 1820	Percifull, Edw.	Alice DeSilvey	
27 Feb. 1833	Percifull, Edw.	Nancy Simmonds	
22 Mch. 1735/6	Perkins, Thos.	Elinor Currell	
16 Dec. 1771	Perkins, Cap. Thos.	Sarah Ann Currell	Dau. of T. Currell
16 Nov. 1724	Phillips, Brian	Eliz. Stott	
3 Sept. 1765	Phillips, Geo.	Mary Yerby	Dau. Eliz. Woodbridge
18 May 1790	Phillips, Wm.	Ellen Carter	
2 Apr. 1823	Phillips, Bern.	Sarah Towill	

Page 51

DATE	GROOM	BRIDE	PARENTS
7 Apr. 1806	Philippine, Hump.	Molly Cox	
1 Oct. 1787	Pickron, Geo. of Northumberland	Mary Billings (widow)	
1 Dec. 1794	Pierce, Ransd, of Westmoreland	Ann Graham	
14 May 1800	Pierce, Stephen	Dorotha Hinton	
23 Feb. 1826	Pierce, Dan. P.	Nancy Robins	
2 Nov. 1830	Pierce, Jos.	Alice M. Tapscott	
17 June 1784	Pinckard, Thos.	Ann Corbin Griffin	
24 Aug. 1805	Pinckard, Edw.	Nancy Meredith	
2 Nov. 1813	Pinckard, Edw.	Eliz. Bradberry	
17 June 1842	Pinckard, Thos.	Ann H. Pollard	
6 Oct. 1787	Pinckard, Geo. of Northumberland	Mary Billings (widow)	
25 Apr. 1789	Pin, Benj. (age 21) (carpenter)	Betty Bell	son of Robt. & Ann Pin dau. of Elias Bell, dec.
3 Mch. 1794	Pinn, Aaron	Mary Kelley Weaver	Dau. Elijah Weaver
19 Apr. 1802	Pinn, Robt.	May Casely	
29 Dec. 1829	Pinn, Wm.	Winney Hill	
23 Feb. 1831	Pinn, Robt.	Roxy Thomas	
21 Jan. 1834	Pinn, James	Dorcas Oliver	
18 Mch. 1847	Pinn, Aaron	Lucy Tankersley	
26 Mch. 1768	Pitman, Isaac	Margaret James	
29 Mch. 1783	Pitman, Jeduthan	Caty Webb	
30 Mch. 1786	Pitman, Thos.	Polly Roberts	
20 Mch. 1788	Pitman, Rd.	Liddy Briscoe Warren	
6 Jan. 1791	Pitman, Thos.	Frances Hill	
15 Oct. 1792	Pitman, Isaac (widower)	Sally White	
17 Dec. 1792	Pitman, James	Nancy Webb (spinster)	Dau. of Rachel Dameron
15 Feb. 1796	Pitman, Burges	Molly Pader Jopes	

Page 52

DATE	GROOM	BRIDE	PARENT
4 Nov. 1801	Pitman, Wm.	Eliz. Hill	
25 Dec. 1803	Pitman, Thos.	Nancy Forester	
1 Jan. 1805	Pitman, Geo. (widower)	Judith Clarke (widow)	
5 Aug. 1807	Pitman, Thos.	Cyntha Hathaway	
11 Jan. 1809	Pitman, Wm.	Polly Dodson	
24 Nov. 1809	Pitman, Wm.	Lida Reveer Beane	
4 Dec. 1817	Pitman, Edw. C.	Mary Rosson	
4 Jan. 1819	Pitman, Isaac	Malinda Hathaway	
12 Apr. 1824	Pitman, Elismond	Sarah Ann Sebree	
11 Jan. 1826	Pitman, Geo.	Alice T. George	
29 Dec. 1825	Pitman, Henry M.	Roxey Kemm	
20 Aug. 1828	Pitman, Leroy M.	Mary Eaton	
24 Dec. 1835	Pittman, Jesse	Eliz. Evins	
18 Dec. 1837	Pitman, Rd.	Mary Ann C. Robinson	
25 Dec. 1839	Pitman, Thos.	Emily M. Doggett	
24 Aug. 1719	Pollard, S ----	Blanche Kelley	
28 Mch. 1762	Pollard, Wm.	Betty Brent	Orphan Hugh Brent
21 Aug. 1797	Pollard, Wm.	Nancy H. George	
28 Sept. 1818	Pollard, Jas.	Catherine P. Brent	
24 Apr. 1765	Pope, Leroy (age 23)	Eliz. Mitchell (age 22)	
22 Jan. 1776	Pope, Nicholas	Eliz. Fleet	Dau. John Fleet
24 Mch. 1796	Pope, Geo.	Fanny McTyre	
20 Apr. 1786	Potts, Thos.	Ann Merryman	
13 May 1802	Potts, John	Sally Chowning	
21 Nov. 1813	Potts, Francis B.	Judith Coates	
12 Jan. 1833	Porter, Wm.	Eliz. H. Brent	
16 Oct. 1762	Powell, Wm.	Nancy Steptoe	
17 June 1784	Prichard, Thos.	Ann Corbin Griffin	

Page 53

DATE	GROOM	BRIDE	PARENTS
16 Dec. 1763	Pullen, Jonathan	Betty Ann Brumley	Dau. of Samuel Brumley
11 Dec. 1782	Pullen, Henry	Hannah Rogers	
17 Nov. 1791	Pullin, Wm.	Hannah Baylie (age 23)	
4 May 1793	Pullen, Thad.	Nancy Findley	
17 Jan. 1795	Pullen, Jonathan of Richmond Co.	Betsy S. Cannon	
10 Jan. 1796	Pullen, Jeduthan	Jane Claughton	
16 Oct. 1797	Pullen, Thad. (widower)	Frances Frizzell Meredith	
15 Jan. 1801	Pullen, Lindsey	Judith Barrett Dameron	
19 Mch. 1811	Pullen, Wm.	Molly Luckham	
1 Jan. 1816	Pullen, Geo.	Sally Warwick	Dau. of Wm. Warwick
17 Dec. 1821	Pullen, Wm.	Amelia Snow	
4 Apr. 1821	Pullen, Jno. B.	Sally B. Currell	
24 Jan. 1844	Pullen, Wm.	Judith C. Fendlee	
18 May 1831	Pursley, Jos. D.	Polly Hutchings	
21 Dec. 1723	Rain, Samuel	Haga Davis	Dau. of John Davis
24 Sept. 1791	Rains, Rawleigh (bachelor)	Peggy Reveer (spinster)	
31 Dec. 1821	Rains, Wm. O.	Nancy M. Morris	
2 Sept. 1843	Redwood, Wm. H.	Catherine C. Chowning	
16 Jan. 1806	Ready, Daniel	Kitty Brown	
25 Dec. 1809	Reese, Daniel	Alice Williams	
14 Aug. 1724	Reeves, Eaton	Priscilla Palmer	
27 Mch. 1781	Reaves, John	Nancy Davis	
17 July 1799	Reaves, Nich.	Lavinia Harrod Lawson	
9 Nov. 1821	Reeves, John	Lucy G. Mason	
3 July 1833	Reaves, Wm.	Jane Alford	
17 Dec. 1771	Riveer, Jno. (younger)	Nancy D. Kirk	

Page 54

DATE	GROOM	BRIDE	PARENTS
28 Dec. 1808	Revere, Jas.	Mary Moore	
13 Nov. 1826	Riveer, Cyrus	Mary Pitman	
7 Dec. 1794	Rheadock, Rd.	Ann Pinn	
18 Dec. 1799	Rice, Peter W.	Eliz. Sampson	
Jan. 1838	Rice, Thos.	Nancy C. Hazzard	
26 Aug. 1786	Rice, David	Hannah Jones	
26 Dec. 1827	Rich, Robt.	Dorrina Laws	
Nov. 1813	Rich, Robt.	Polly Wood	
14 Dec. 1828	Rich, Thad.	Judith Nickins	
31 Dec. 1777	Richards, John	Mary Hunton	
8 May 1788	Richards, Lewis	Lucy Hunton	Dau. of Thos. Hunton
29 Oct. 1784	Richardson, John	Mary Wilson	
9 Jan. 1733	Robbs, Jas.	Frances Buckles	
7 Jan. 1794	Rob, James	Judith Carter (widow)	
22 Dec. 1803	Robb, Jas.	Caty Bailey	
4 Feb. 1780	Roberts, John	Eliz. Mehone	
16 July 1787	Roberts, John	Mary Longwith	
8 Mch. 1812	Roberts, John	Caty George	
1 Dec. 1825	Roberts, John	Mary A. Wilder	
27 Feb. 1846	Roberts, Jos. G.	Henrietta Berry Mitchell	
27 Nov. 1758	Robertson, Andrew	Ellen Chichester	
28 Jan. 1800	Robertson, Robt. M.	Jane Newton Brent	
11 Dec. 1801	Robertson, Thos. G.	Lettice L. Brent	
30 May 1809	Robertson, Andrew	Catherine L. Brent	
20 Apr. 1835	Robertson, Andrew	Sidney T. Hathaway	
20 Apr. 1797	Robins, Archib.	Mary Meredith (widow)	
21 Aprl 1800	Robins, Jesse	Alice Burges Hinton	
19 Sept. 1803	Robins, Elijah	Priscilla Robinson	

Page 55

DATE	GROOM	BRIDE	PARENTS
6 Mch. 1838	Robbins, John	Sarah Hinton under age	Dau. of Archib. Hinton
21 May 1764	Robinson, Jesse of Northumberland	Lucy Rob	
30 Oct. 1773	Robinson, John	Margaret Heid (spinster)	
14 Jan. 1779	Robinson, Jesse	Aggy Norris	
22 July 1785	Robinson, Epaph.	Milly Chilton	
29 Mch. 1786	Robinson, James	Winny Taff	
27 Apr. 1787	Robinson, Jesse	Polly Coffee	
8 Jan. 1791	Robinson, Moses	Fanny Robinson	
18 Sept. 1794	Robinson, Epaph.	Betsy Everitt	
24 Jan. 1797	Robinson, Wm. M.	Nancy Sullivant	
9 May 1800	Robinson, Epaph.	Betty Morrison	
4 May 1808	Robinson, Moses	Betsy Kemm	Gr.dau. of Jas. Towles
23 Oct. 1810	Robinson, James	Lucinda G. Thaikill	
31 Dec. 1811	Robinson, Cyrus	Lucy Alford	
29 Dec. 1817	Robinson, Moses	Fanny Dunaway	
8 Aug. 1828	Robinson, Moses	Beheth. N. George	
11 Dec. 1833	Robinson, Wm.	Margaret Sullivan	
16 May 1836	Robinson, Joel	Emily Cundiff	
7 Feb. 1839	Robinson, Josiah	Maria Brown	
14 Dec. 1840	Robinson, Nelson	Frances I. Hutchings	
21 May 1849	Robinson, Wm.	Mary Thrift	
9 June 1849	Robinson, John	Caroline H. Bradley	
14 Sept. 1796	Rock, Chas.	Winifred Lee of Northumberland Co.	Los. Locke uncle of bride
16 Feb. 1786	Roderick, Anthony	Eliz. Reaves	
23 Aug. 1723	Rogers, John	Jane Walters (widow)	
21 Sept. 1750	Rogers, Edward of Northumberland	Katherine Edmonds	

DATE	GROOM	BRIDE	PARENTS
25 Apr. 1775	Rogers, Chas.	Peggy Chowning	
20 Mch. 1762	Rogers, Chas.	Katherine Brent	Dau. of Wm. Carter's wife
10 Mch. 1796	Rogers, Chas.	Judith Hathaway	
9 Dec. 1813	Rogers, Wm. H.	Mary Page Carter	Dau. of Jos. Carter, Jr.
2 Feb. 1827	Rogers, Chas.	Mary Ann Myers	
7 Dec. 1827	Rogers, George	Olivia Norris	
19 July 1832	Rogers, Chas.	Margaret Ann Chilton	
7 May 1839	Rogers, Chas. W.	Eliz. Ann Saunders	
7 May 1848	Rogers, John	Lavalia T. Hudson	
27 Jan. 1814	Routt, Rd. D.	Sally Bush	
5 Apr. 1796	Row, Wm. C.	Ann Lee	
11 Jan. 1847	Rowe, Wm.	Sarah Ann Garner	Dau. of Griffin Garner
27 Aug. 1771	Rowland, Thos.	Mary Kenner (spinster)	Dau. of Brereton Kenner
21 Apr. 1808	Sampson, John	Molly Cundiff	
18 Sept. 1783	Saunders, Presly	Winny Kent	
23 Nov. 1820	Saunders, Wm.	Harriett Kirk	
19 Mch. 1835	Saunders, Rd.	Alice M. Chilton	
Mch. 1836	Saunders, Anthony	Judith A. Currell	
Oct. 1846	Saunders, John M.	Lucy F. E. Cox	Dau. of John H. Cox
18 Feb. 1833	Savis, Rd. H.	Alice Hayden	
14 Jan. 1791	Scurlock, Geo., Jr.	Frankie Boid age over 21	
9 Jan. 1762	Schofield, Wm.	Judith Purcell	Son of Wm. Schofield
8 Apr. 1792	Schofield, Thos. born May 8, 1770	Catherine George	Son of Wm. Schofield Dau. of Catherine George
10 June 1796	Schofield, Thos.	Betsy Clayton	
26 Dec. 1803	Schofield, Henry	Polly Tapscott	Dau. of Ezekiel Tapscott

Page 57

DATE	GROOM	BRIDE	PARENTS
Feb. 1831	Schofield, Thos.	Lucy Hinton	
Jan. 1834	Schofield, Shap.	Ann M. E. Ashburn	Dau. of Jas. Ashburn
2 Apr. 1730	Scott, Thos.	Susanna Odoe (widow)	
June 1825	Scringer, Wm.	Alice B. Williams	
Apr. 1737	Scrosby, Jas. of Middlesex Co.	Eliz. Lee widow of Thos. Lee	
1796	Sebree, Jesse	Delilah Riveer	
19 June 1797	Sebree, John	Mary Fraser	
20 Mch. 1798	Sebree, Tarpley	Hannah Thomas	
17 Dec. 1798	Sebree, Nicholas	Betty Barnes Marsh b. 10 July 1777	Dau. of Gideon and Molly Marsh
14 Nov. 1821	Sebree, Henry B.	Eliz. Cundiff	Dau. of Jno. Cundiff
22 Dec. 1823	Sebree, Travis	Dealy Church	
8 Mch. 1826	Sebree, John	Peggy Dudley	
20 Apr. 1829	Sebree, Jas.	Delia G. Davis	
13 May 1829	Sebry, Robt.	Winnie Ann Sebry	
21 July 1834	Sebree Moses	Parmelia Davis	
20 May 1836	Sebree, Jos.	Frances Thrift	
30 Aug. 1794	Selbay, Wm.	Lucy Chilton	Jemima, now wife of Thos. Cox and late wife of Thos. Chilton, dec, father of bride
1 Sept. 1794	Selbay, Wm.	Molly Brown	Dau. of Molly Brown
5 Feb. 1807	Selby, Wm.	Eliz. Flemming	
14 Oct. 1725	Selden, John of Eliz. City Co.	Mrs. Sarah Ball	Dau. Rd. Ball
21 Nov. 1741	Selden, Rd.	Mrs. Mary Ball	Son of Jno. Selden Dau. of Jas. Ball
7 May 1766	Selden, Jas.	Mildred Ball	Dau. of Jas. Ball
14 June 1803	Selden, Rd.	Eliz. Nutt	
29 Dec. 1794	Settles, Wm.	Nancy Blakemore	

Page 58

DATE	GROOM	BRIDE	PARENTS
13 Feb. 1810	Settle, Wm.	Mary Chowning	Cons. of Wm. Chowning
27 Dec. 1819	Settle, Wm. E.	Lucy Payne	Wm. Oldham, gd. of bride
3 Sept. 1806	Seward, John	Eliz. Chinn	
Jan. 1829	Jno. widower	Frances Lee	
7 Jan. 1840	Shay, Martin	Penelope Pursell	Dau. of Jno. Pursell
27 Sept. 1845	Shackelford, Edwin	Eliz. Pierce	Dau. of L. Pierce
17 Nov. 1794	Sheardock, Rd.	Ann Pinn	
29 June 1756	Shearman, Rawl.	Eliz. Gilbert	Orphan Ezekiel Gilbert,
7 Jan. 1762	Shearman, Martin	Mary Hunt	Dau. Eliz. Stott
10 Mch. 1768	Shearman, Jos.	Susanna Chinn	Sister of Robt. Chinn
23 Feb. 1784	Shearman, Martin	Alice Tapscott	
7 June 1794	Shearman, Thos.	Molly Bailey	
5 Oct. 1801	Shearman, Sam. M.	Nancy Martin	
10 Feb. 1806	Shearman, Jos.	Lavinia Shearman	
19 Apr. 1807	Shearman, Jos.	Betsy M. Steptoe	
14 July 1808	Shearman, Ezek.	Betsy Tapscott	
17 Dec. 1817	Shearman, Thos.	Eliz. Mitchell	
2 Mch. 1819	Shearman, Jos.	Caroline Meredith	
27 May 1840	Shearman, Ezek. G.	Eliz. M. R. James	
24 Sept. 1788	Shilton, Rd. Step.	Nancy Kent	
22 Apr. 1790	Shelton, Thos.	Caty Payne	Dau. Bridget Payne
15 Jan. 1823	Shelton, John P.	Sally M. C. George	
18 Mch. 1794	Sherburne, H. S.	Joanna Hutchinson (widow)	
7 Jan. 1788	Short, Thos.	Liddy Carter	Dau. of Ann Carter
20 July 1801	Short, Thos.	Eliz. Cox (widow)	
17 May 1817	Short, Moses	Eliz.	
23 Dec. 1830	Short		

Page 59

DATE	GROOM	BRIDE	PARENTS
22 May 1847	Sibruk, Jno. Y.	Eliza A. Towles	
3 Jan. 1769	Simmons, Jas.	Eliz. Hammonds	
8 Apr. 1799	Simmonds, John	Sinah Mahanes	Dau. of Meredith Mahanes
17 Aug. 1801	Simmonds, Wm.	Frances Robb	
21 Jan. 1811	Simmonds, Chas.	Lucy T. George	
20 Dec. 1832	Simmonds, Chas.	Susan Kemm	
26 Dec. 1839	Simmonds, Chas.	Sarah Brent	
28 June 1804	Sims, Wm.	Kathy Percifull	
21 Apr. 1834	Sims, Jas.	Eliza Haydon	
30 Apr. 1850	Sims, John	Judith E. D. Carter	
30 Mch. 1787	Smock, Jas.	Sarah Hunton	
16 June 1781	Smallwood, John	Lucy Fleet	
Feb. 1728/9	Smith, Rev. Chas. of Northumberland	Eliz. Chilton	
26 Nov. 1743	Smith, Baldwin	Frances Burgess	
5 Dec. 1748	Smith, Baldwin M. of Northumberland	Mrs. Frances Burgess	
23 Mch. 1754	Smith, John	Ann Neasum	
27 July 1785	Smith, Wm.	Eliz. Burn	
20 Dec. 1791	Smith, Jno. Mat. Bachelor	Sarah Y. Chinn spinster	
15 Aug. 1794	Smith, Wm.	Catherine King	
23 Sept. 1813	Smith, Geo.	Milly Merriman	
23 Feb. 1835	Smith, Gilbert	Rocksey Clarke	
8 Feb. 1840	Smith, John	Margaret Ann Boatman	Dau. of John Boatman
26 Nov. 1840	Smith, Robt. H.	Catherine L. Hunt	Dau. of Lucinda Hunt
25 Feb. 1846	Smith, Robt. W.	Catherine George	Dau. of Zamoth George
11 Nov. 1761	Smither, John	Lucy Carter	Dau. of Thos. Carter
5 Aug. 1803	Smither, Wm.	Eliz. Lawson	

Page 60

DATE	GROOM	BRIDE	PARENTS
14 Jan. 1805	Smither, Geo.	Ann F. Spiller	
20 July 1762	Snale, Capt. Thos.	Eliz. Weathers Haynes	Orph. Jas. Haynes, Jr.
2 May 1808	Snow, John	Lucy Gartin	
15 Dec. 1814	Sorrell, Edw. of Northumberland	Dacris Lewin	
14 Dec. 1819	Sorrell, Martin	Judith Causy	
22 Aug. 1836	Spann, John	Eliz. A. Doggett	
1 Apr. 1779	Spilman, Joshua	Mary Ayliff	
6 Feb. 1794	Spilman, Joshua (widower)	Barbara Dameron (widow)	
22 Dec. 1803	Spilman, Wm.	Eliz. Lunsford	Dau. Jane Lunsford
23 May 1809	Spilman, Geo.	Alice Yopp	
2 Feb. 1835	Spilman, Wm.	Eliz. Greenwood	
22 Apr. 1841	Spilman, Stokes S.	Lucy C. Chilton	
1 Oct. 1787	Spriggs, Ephraim	Lucy Flowers (widow)	Bro. of Nathan Spriggs
2 June 1788	Spriggs, Nathan	Sarah Hutchings	
18 Jan. 1802	Spriggs, Ephraim	Sarah Hammond	
27 Dec. 1824	Spriggs, Jos.	Winny Spriggs	Dau. of Nathan Spriggs
21 May 1829	Spriggs, Nathan	Nancy Spriggs	
6 Nov. 1750	Stamps, Wm.	Eliner Brent, Jr.	Dau. Catherine Brent
21 Feb. 1717	Stevens, Chris.	Mary Arnes (widow)	
12 June 1728	Stevens, Jos.	Judah Davenport	Cousin of Geo. Davenport
20 Dec. 1756	Stephens, Rd.	Frances Payne	Dau. of Geo. Payne
15 Mch. 1782	Stephens, Jos.	Charlotte Brent	
15 Oct. 1787	Stephens, Geo. of Orange Co.	Priscilla Brent	
23 Mch. 1789	Stephens, John	Eliz. Cornelius age 23	Consent of Wm. Cornelius
19 Dec. 1808	Stephens, Rd.	Frances Mott	
25 Jan. 1819	Stephens, Geo.	Eliz. B. George	

Page 61

DATE	GROOM	BRIDE	PARENTS
4 Dec. 1822	Stephens, Rd. A.	Alcinda Woody	
7 May 1824	Stephens, Wm. E.	Catherine Minter	
27 May 1848	Stephens, Jos.	Margaret Peirce	
10 June 1727	Steptoe, John	Joanna Lawson	Dau. Jean Lawson
4 Jan. 1764	Steptoe, Wm. of Northumberland	Betty Woodbridge Yerby	Dau. Geo. Yerby
5 Oct. 1772	Steptoe, Wm.	Joanna Doggett	
12 Dec. 1786	Steptoe, John	Eliz. Martin George	
18 Mch. 1765	Stott, Thos.	Bettie Stoneham	
25 Dec. 1780	Stott, Oliver of Richmond Co.	Molly Harris	
19 Sept. 1786	Stott, Oliver	Eliz. Norris	
19 Oct. 1786	Stott, Rd.	Nancy Bush	
9 July 1804	Stott, Rd.	Polly C. Newsome	
17 Apr. 1797	Stott, Wm.	Sarah F. Hinton	
6 May 1813	Stott, John S.	Alcy Davis	
1 June 1816	Stott, John S.	Mrs. Rebecca M. Thrall	
11 Nov. 1822	Stott, Jasper	Mary Ann Miller	
22 May 1826	Stott, Jasper	Eliz. Yerby	
3 Apr. 1829	Stott, Barthol.	Eliz. Fallin	
20 Dec. 1830	Stott, Wm. H.	Fanny B. Mitchell	
5 Dec. 1817	Stoneham, Sam.	Eliz. R. Palmer	
18 Feb. 1850	Stoneham, Rd. A.	Eliz. Jane Lee	
10 Apr. 1828	Stoneham, Hiram	Mary H. Yerby	
	Stover, Jos.	Judith Davenport	Dau. of Geo. Davenport
20 Mch. 1821	Strachan, R. C.	Eliz. H. A. Currie	Dau. of E. Currie
11 Jan. 1849	Straughan, Sam. L.	Marian L. Lawson	
20 Nov. 1834	Strother, Geo. W.	Sarah S. Chowning	
19 Jan. 1787	Sutton, Saml.	Winifred Cundiff	

DATE	GROOM	BRIDE	PARENTS
24 Sept. 1792	Sutton, Jas.	Mary Cundiff	Son of Moses Sutton
11 Oct. 1790	Sullivan, Wm.	Eliz. Fendley	
3 July 1794	Sullivan, Wm.(widower)	Caty Ward (widow)	
12 July 1815	Sullivan, Thos. of Northumberland	Sally Cundiff	Dau. of Jno. Cundiff
23 Dec. 1833	Sullivan, Corne	Mary Sampson	
20 Feb. 1843	Sullivan, Jas. V.	Ann Stonum	
11 June 1845	Sullivant, Robt.	Eliz. Dunnaway	
2 July 1779	Sullivant, John	Mary Nichols	
25 Feb. 1808	Sullivant, Hiram	Nancy Stonum	
29 Dec. 1836	Summers, Hugh	Sarah Ann Hammond	Dau. of Wm. Hammond
15 Feb. 1796	Swaine, Wm.	Charlotte Sebra	
28 Jan. 1822	Swaine, Wm.	Catherine Talley	
28 July 1791	Swanson, Asa (widower)	Betty H. Garton	Dau. Milly Garton
Apr. 1840	Swanson, Cyrus	Margaret Dameron	
3 Jan. 1736	Sydnor, Anthony	Eliz. Taylor	Son of Wm. & Cath. Taylor
1 Jan. 1788	Sydnor, Anthony	Eliz. Hinton	
7 Jan. 1788	Sydnor, Anthony	Eliz. Chowning	
16 Feb. 1848	Sidnor, Eppa	Jane Nickens	
16 Dec. 1715	Sydnor, Wm.	Rachel Davenport	
	Sydnor, Wm.	Catherine Taylor	
	Sydnor, Fortun.	Eliz. Sharpe	
10 Mch. 1813	Sydnor, Wm.	Margaret S. Brent	
14 Feb. 1817	Sydnor, Wm.	Mary Kirk	Dau. of Wm. Kirk
26 Dec. 1808	Taff, John	Eliz. Dodson	
10 June 1839	Tankard, Jno. W.	Susan W. Taylor	Dau. of Thorowgood Taylor
11 Feb. 1758	Tapscott, Henry	Mary Shearman	
16 Feb. 1762	Tapscott, Edney	Mary Waugh	

Page 63

DATE	GROOM	BRIDE	PARENTS
---Aug. 1783	Tapscott, Rawl.	Ann Shearman	
16 June 1786	Tapscott, Martin	Mary Rowand	
8 Sept. 1786	Tapscott, John	Mary Spilman	
14 Aug. 1789	Tapscott, Rd.	Frances George	Dau. of Frances George
19 Feb. 1810	Tapscott, Henry	Sarah Yopp	
1 July 1829	Tapscott, Henry	Alcey Cundiff	
19 Feb. 1829	Tapscott, Jos.	Eliz. T. Hutchings	
11 Sept. 1832	Tapscott, Robt.	Olivia Degge	
15 Oct. 1832	Tapscott, Jos.	Mary M. Mitchell	Dau. of Geo. M. Mitchel
16 Feb. 1835	Tapscott, Jos.	Margaret C. Doggett	
23 Dec. 1848	Tapscott, Henry	--------	
19 Jan. 1796	Tally, Geo.	Nancy Pitman	
27 Mch. 1796	Tally, Thos. J.	Hannah Webb	
13 Nov. 1796	Tally, John, Jr.	Jemima Webb	
4 Sept. 1806	Tally, Champion	Nancy C. Cornish	Son of John Tally
1 Jan. 1816	Tally, Jas.	Nancy Robinson	
11 Dec. 1827	Tally, Geo.	Lucy Selvey	
10 June 1828	Tally, Thos.	Mary Chilton	
20 Sept. 1833	Tally, Dan. L.	Polly Palmer	
16 Dec. 1836	Tally, Jas.	Virginia Stimson	
16 Dec. 1793	Tarkleson, Tarkel	Margaret Thatcher	
10 Nov. 1840	Tayloe, Thos.	Lucy Boyd	
12 Dec. 1741	Taylor, Thos.	Mrs. Eve Ball	Dau. of Jas. Ball
8 Aug. 1785	Taylor, Isaac	Eliz. Carter	
2 Oct. 1823	Tebbs, Foushee G.	Sarah Downman	
Feb. 1798	Thatcher, Geo.	Milly Haydon	
5 July 1784	Thomas, Rhodem	Eliz. Wilkerson	
10 Oct. 1805	Trekle, Dempsey b. Aug. 28, 1784	Martha Wheeler widow	Rd. Trekle, father

Page 64

DATE	GROOM	BRIDE	PARENTS
May 1808	Thomas, Vincent	Sukey Bean	
11 Feb. 1821	Thomas, Vincent	Sally Bean	
4 Dec. 1826	Thomas, John	Mrs. Mary Gains	
1828	Thomas, John W.	Margaret Sebry	
1831	Thomas, Griffin E.	Nancy Webb	
1834	Thomas, Washington	Mary Oliver	
1839	Thomas, Leroy	Harriett Rich	Dau. of Eppa Rich
1790	Thrailkill, Linds	Ann Stonum	
1789	Thrall, John	Ellen George	
1 Feb. 1809	Thrall, Thos.	Rebecca M. George	
17 Dec. 1810	Thrall, John, Jr.	Judith Clarke	
28 Oct. 1835	Thrall, Jas.	Ann Carpenter	
4 June 1833	Thrift, John F.	Eliza Douglas	
4 June 1835	Thrift, Thos.	Judith Thomas	
27 Nov. 1841	Thrift, Thos.	Margaret Ann Doggett	
22 Dec. 1846	Thrift, John F.	Ann E. Bloxom	
9 Mch. 1730	Timberlake, Fran.	Judith Lawson	
26 Nov. 1846	Toby, Thos. W.	Isabelle Hall	
15 Dec. 1806	Toleman, John	Susannah Williams	
5 Jan. 1782	Towell, Mark	Ann Hunton	
17 Mch. 1808	Towell, Thos.	Ann Currell Lee under 21	Dau. of Thos. Lee
26 Sept. 1811	Towell, Rd.	Sally Hinton	
12 Mch. 1736	Towles, Stokely	Eliz. Martin	Kath. Brent mother of bride
19 May 1768	Towles, Henry	Judith Haynes	
21 May 1795	Towles, Henry, Jr. (mariner)	Alice Chilton	
21 Jan. 1799	Towles, Stokely	Mary W. Ball	
18 Feb. 1802	Towles, Porteus	Frances Towles	

Page 65

DATE	GROOM	BRIDE	PARENTS
8 Oct. 1807	Towles, Jas.	Felicia Chowning	
14 June 1809	Towles, Oliver	Margaret Yerby	Only dau. of Wm. Yerby
8 Mch. 1815	Towles, Wm. P.	Lucy W. Degge	
9 Sept. 1822	Towles, Thos.	Kitturah George	
13 Aug. 1833	Towles, Jas. S.	Sarah L. Towles	
30 July 1835	Towles, John	Sophronia E. Chowning	Consent of J. C. Chowning
25 Dec. 1843	Towles, Oliver	Louisa C. George	
15 Dec. 1818	Travers, Wm.	Chloe Ingram	Dau. Mary Ingram
10 Oct. 1805	Treackle, Dempsey	Martha Wheeler (widow)	Son of Rd. Treackle
4 Nov. 1805	Treakle, Saml.	Judith Williams	
23 Dec. 1823	Treackle, Wm.	Judith Bottoms	
13 June 1828	Treakle, Jno. S.	Frances Hutchinson	
16 Dec. 1829	Treakle, Jno. R.	Eliz. B. Hutchinson	
15 Oct. 1836	Treakle, Jas. W.	Louisa B. Bridgeman	
15 May 1837	Treakle, Wm.	Eliz. Yerby	
17 Apr. 1838	Treakle, Dempsey	Mary Ashburn above 21 yrs.	
29 July 1841	Treakle, Wm. T.	Eliza Gaines	
25 Apr. 1844	Treakle, John K.	Polly Hughlett	
20 Apr. 1846	Treakle, Jas.	Mary Ann Yerby	
15 July 1848	Treakle, Jas. W.	Mary Dameron	
12 Mch. 1833	Trott, Alex.	Sally George	
23 Jan. 1834	Trott, Benj.	Clary P. Doggett	
11 Feb. 1811	Tuck, Jos.	Patsy Bradberry	
3 Oct. 1791	Tucker, St. Geo. of Williamsburg	Mrs. Lelia Carter (widow)	
20 Dec. 1825	Tune, Travis D.	Jane Stott	
19 July 1845	Turner, Benj.	Eliz. Henderson	
6 Dec. 1826	Tycer, Saml.	Alice Riveer	

Page 66

DATE	GROOM	BRIDE	PARENTS
15 Jan. 1824	Vanlandingham, Geo.	Eliz. W. Cockerall	
17 June 1844	Vanlandingham, Man.	Eliz. Dozier	
9 Nov. 1837	Vanness, Julius	Ann B. Forrester	
29 Apr. 1841	Vanness, Isaac	Mary L. Hunt	
1 Apr. 1806	Vaughan, John	Chloe Hubbard	Dau. of Judith Hubbard
5 May 1818	Veney, Simon	Betsy Laws	
16 June 1831	Venea, Rd.	Judith Vanes	
24 Mch. 1834	Veney, Robt.	Luky Watkins	
17 Feb. 1849	Veney, James	Lucy Nickens	
11 Jan. 1821	Vowell, Val. H.	Eliz. T. James	
7 Oct. 1767	Waddell, Rev. Jas.	Mary Gordon	Dau. of Jas. Gordon
5 Dec. 1766	Waddy, Benj. of Northumberland	Margaret Payne	
1 Oct. 1770	Waddy, Jas.	Hannah Edwards (widow)	
29 Oct. 1779	Waddy, Jesse	Mary Taylor	
14 Jan. 1796	Waddy, Geo.	Eliz. Maxwell	
27 Nov. 1817	Waddy, Benj.	Jannette P. Edmonds	
20 Sept. 1819	Waddy, John	Delia Yerby	
14 May 1783	Wale, Lawson	Winifred Spriggs	
11 Apr. 1777	Walker, Robt.	Sarah Ann Sebree	
7 Jan. 1796	Walker, Jos.	Jane Newby	
11 Nov. 1807	Walker, Jos. D.	Lilly G. Schofield	
20 Feb. 1815	Walker, Pressly	Sally K. Cottrell	
24 Feb. 1820	Walker, John	Leannah Treacle	
2 Jan. 1822	Walker, Benj.	Lucy Simmons	
15 Jan. 1823	Walker, John	Betsy Wheeler	
22 Dec. 1824	Walker, Baldsin	Sarah Chilton	
9 May 1827	Walker, Presley	Ann Jefferson	

Page 67

DATE	GROOM	BRIDE	PARENTS
4 Dec. 1837	Walker, Thos. C.	Mary C. George	
15 Mch. 1841	Walker, Geo. S.	Ellinor H. Forester	
27 Mch. 1843	Walker, Jos. R.	Mary R. Chilton	
15 July 1848	Walker, Wm.	Mrs. Harriet Gundra	
23 Dec. 1801	Waide, Robt. C.	Alice M. George	
20 Jan. 1814	Wall, Saml.	Ellen Dameron	Dau. of Polly Dameron
28 Jan. 1815	Wall, Rd.	Nancy Newby	Dau. Wm. Newby
15 June 1829	Wall, John R.	Janet James	
25 July 1780	Wallace, Jas.	Grace Walker	
10 Feb. 1789	Wallace, Wm.	Judith Walker	Dau. of Mary Walker
4 Feb. 1850	Ward, Thos. R.	Zepporah A. Flowers	
4 Sept. 1787	Warwick, Philip	Ann Stott	Dau. of Eliz. Stott
25 Jan. 1792	Warwick, Benj.	Charlotte George	
15 Sept. 1794	Warwick, Wm.	Eleanor Garner	Widow of Wm. Garner
31 July 1797	Warwick, Geo.	Ann Edney George	
9 Jan. 1718	Warwick, Thos.	Jane Brown	
23 Nov. 1820	Warwick, Jas.	Ann De Silve	
28 May 1822	Warwick, Wm.	Eliz. Ashburno	
22 Feb. 1825	Warwick, Philip	Nancy Stott	
27 May 1826	Warwick, Jas.	Polly Thrift	
9 June 1838	Warwick, John	Mary Arms	
20 Apr. 1849	Warwick, Jas. R.	Margaret Swanson	
10 Dec. 1849	Warwick, Jas. W.	Mary E. Trice	
15 Oct. 1850	Warwick, Benj. P.	Olivia R. Taylor	
10 Dec. 1829	Waters, Wm. E. of Somerset, Md.	Augustina C. Humphries	
6 Apr. 1829	Waters, Thos. L.	Ann L. Towell	
26 Jan. 1797	Watts, John	Bridget Payne	

DATE	GROOM	BRIDE	PARENTS
30 Mch. 1801	Watts, Spencer	Betsy Butler	
6 June 1826	Watts, John E.	Ann Kellum	
5 Oct. 1831	Watts, Ewell	Rebecca Carter	
11 Sept. 1805	Wayman, John	Lucinda Blakemore	
10 June 1789	Weaver, John	Dorcas Bell	
7 July 1794	Weaver, Thos.	Eliza Lawes	
28 Nov. 1811	Weaver, Henry	Jenny Weaver	
31 Dec. 1816	Weaver, Moses	Janette Smith	Dau. of Sally Mactear
7 Dec. 1830	Weaver, Thos.	Eliz. Dunaway	Dau. of Eliz. Dunaway
7 Sept. 1844	Weaver, Moses	Arabella Thornton	
6 Mch. 1769	Webb, Jas.	Mary Holder	
21 Sept. 1789	Webb, Wm.	Patty Hill	
30 Sept. 1786	Webb, Thos.	Judith Raisey	
20 Feb. 1795	Webb, Thos.	Molly Boatman	
6 June 1795	Webb, Chas.	Mary Sullivant (widow)	
9 Feb. 1797	Webb, Thos. (widower)	Mary Tally (spinster)	
31 May 1804	Webb, Chas.	Sally Overstreet	
27 Dec. 1808	Webb, Geo.	Alice Tapscott	Wm. Kelly, Sec. Declares bride to be of age
5 June 1817	Webb, Jos.	Priscilla Doggett	
20 Dec. 1819	Webb, James	Rebecca Percifull	
15 Mch. 1820	Webb, Geo.	Polly N. Neale	
28 July 1835	Webb, Jos.	Catherine Dunaway	
16 Feb. 1841	Webb, Jos.	Eliza Ann Brown	
24 Dec. 1845	Webb, Jas. R.	Mary C. Ingram	
20 Dec. 1844	Webb, Jos.	Eliz. Thomas	Dau. of Susan Thomas
3 June 1849	Webb, John	Frances R. Talley	
17 Nov. 1842	Wessell, Custis	Nancy Mason	

Page 69

DATE	GROOM	BRIDE	PARENTS
20 June 1735	West, Robt. (bricklayer)	Margaret Buckles of Christ Church	
24 Nov. 1802	West, Jos.	Betsy Chitwood	
16 Dec. 1816	West, Jos.	Betsy Toleman	
24 Feb. 1841	West, James	Huldah Hammond	
22 Dec. 1848	West, James	Eliz. Hammond	
4 June 1737	Wharton, Jos.	Ann Edmunds	Dau. of Elias Edmunds
30 May 1799	Wheeler, Moses	Martha Williams	
11 Oct. 1727	White, Isaac	Mary Ann Ewell	
31 Dec. 1793	White, Griffin	Polly Demeritt	
17 Mch. 1788	Wiblin, Wm.	Sarah Beavens	
2 Feb. 1803	Wilcox, James	Nancy Hill 24 yrs. old	
18 May 1780	Wilder, Michael	Ann Carter	
31 Jan. 1786	Wilder, Geo.	Sukey Davis	
30 May 1789	Wilder, Spencer	Sally Yopp	
8 May 1793	Wilder, John (bachelor)	Lucy Webb (spinster)	
27 Nov. 1793	Wilder, Michael	Mary McColly	
18 Mch. 1794	Wilder, Jonathan	Mary Overstreet	
17 Mch. 1794	Wilder, Newman	Nancy George b. 12 Mch. 1772	Dau. of Harry George
15 June 1824	Wilder, Michael, Jr.	Nancy Hammond	Dau. of Nancy Hammond
17 Dec. 1850	Wilder, John	Eliz. Hurst	
25 Sept. 1792	Williams, Peter	Alcy Connelly	Dau. Patrick Connelly
16 Oct. 1792	Williams, John	Molly Ballay	
28 Sept. 1798	Williams, John	Sarah Mason	
17 Dec. 1798	Williams, Wm.	Sarah Cornelius	
29 Nov. 1827	Williams, Jas. C.	Lucy C. Hutchings	
6 Jan. 1835	Williams, Peter	Leannah Doggett	

DATE	GROOM	BRIDE	PARENTS
21 Nov. 1843	Williams, Peter	Mary Ann Beane	
11 Apr. 1849	Williams, John S.	Jane Bottoms	
19 Jan. 1791	Wilson, Wm.	Molly Taylor Schofield	
21 Dec. 1814	Wilson, Cyrus	Olivia Stott	
3 Oct. 1836	Winstead, Lucius S. of Northumberland	Eliz. S. Pitman	
20 Jan. 1813	Wood, Thos.	Sally Bee	
17 Sept. 1821	Wood, John	Janetta Hutchens	
15 Oct. 1821	Wood, Holland	Jane Haw	
30 May 1833	Wood, Thos.	Nancy Cox.	Dau. of Patty Cox
14 Jan. 1834	Wood, Holland	Sally Wood	
1731	Woodson, John of Goochland	Mary Miller	Dau. of Wm. Miller
Feb. 21, 1818	Woody, Thos.	Alcinda Kid	
23 Dec. 1828	Woody, John	Ann A. Herron	
1746	Wormley, John of Middlesex	Mrs. Ann Tayloe of Christ Church Parish.	Dau. of Wm. Tayloe
Aug. 19, 1789	Wormley, John	Fanny Bond	
1808	Wornam, Geo.	Lucy Hubbard	Dau. of Lucy Hubbard
14 June, 1829	Wornam, Thos.	Lucy Kirkham	Dau. of John Kirkham
19 Jan. 1809	Wornam, Thos.	Ann C. Chowning	
10 Jan. 1833	Wornam, Thos. W.	Eliz. Sebree	
Dec. 26, 1833	Wornam, Chas.	Julia A. Webb	
	Wren, Wm.	Joanna George	
24 Dec. 1783	Wyatt, John	Mary Harwood Currell	
1717	Yerby, Thos.	Hannah Doggett	
	Yerby, Geo.	Eliz. Meredith	
19 June, 1815	Yerby, Chas.	Jane Pidsly Towell	Dau. of Mark Towell
16 Jan. 1786	Yerby, Rd.	Judith George	

DATE	GROOM	BRIDE	PARENTS
1753	Yerby, Wm.	Frances McTire	Dau. Robt. McTire
	Yerby, Chas. J.	Sally Chilton	Dau. Judith Chilton
7 Apr. 1823	Yerby, Ellyson	Hannah Meredith	
7 March, 1827	Yerby, Wm.	Eliz. B. Wilson	
14 Jan. 1824	Yerby, Wm.	Harriett Beane	Dau. of Opie Beane
23 Feb. 1829	Yerby, Wm.	Cordelia Chilton	
17 Mch. 1835	Yerby, Jas. W.	Catherine Bayse	
Dec. 7, 1842	Yerby, Chas. H.	Margaret George	Dau. Zamoth George
July 3, 1754	Yopp, Saml.	Mary Simmons	Dau. Eliz. Simmons
Apr. 1782	Yopp, Saml.	Molly Dogget	

www.ingramcontent.com/pod-product-compliance
Lightning Source LLC
Chambersburg PA
CBHW071230160426
43196CB00012B/2463